Real Fast
Vegetarian Food

Real Fast Vegetarian Food

Ursula Ferrigno

edited by Susanna Tee

Published by Metro Publishing Ltd, 3 Bramber Court, 2 Bramber
Road, London W14 9PB, England

ISBN 1 84358 007 1

British Library Cataloguing-in-Publication Data: A catalogue
record for this book is available from the British Library.

Typeset by SX Composing DTP, Rayleigh, Essex
Illustrations by Madeleine Hardie

Printed and bound in Great Britain by CPD (Wales)

1 3 5 7 9 10 8 6 4 2

Papers used by Metro Publishing Ltd are natural, recyclable
products made from wood grown in sustainable forests. The
manufacturing processes conform to the environmental
regulations of the country of origin.

Ursula Ferrigno was born in Southern Italy to an Italian father and English mother and grew up in an environment where family life was centred around the kitchen table. The quality and taste of food was of paramount importance and her enthusiasm for cooking continued after her move to England, where she went on to become a professional chef. Ursula set up the first vegetarian restaurant in north west England and its success prompted Ursula to try her hand at writing.

Her first book, *The 90's Vegetarian*, published in 1994, contains recipes inspired by the Mediterranean and a year later Ursula wrote her second book, *Pizza, Pasta and Polenta*.

As well as her work as a writer, Ursula is a passionate cookery teacher. She was the principal tutor for The Vegetarian Society, head teacher at The Cordon Vert Cookery School and now runs highly successful courses at the Books for Cooks Cookery School as well as in Italy. She is a frequent demonstrator at the BBC Good Food Shows and has become a valued food consultant for a number of major companies. Ursula is also a regular television and radio broadcaster.

Dedication

To my Grandmother who works miracles in the kitchen.

Acknowledgements

I am extremely grateful to –

FIONA LINDSAY and LINDA SHANKS, my Agents, for their great
work and persistence with my career.
SUSANNA TEE for editing my book and working beyond the call of
duty. I am enormously grateful.
JENNY AND DAVE ROBERTS of Premier Services for deciphering
my scribbles, and endless amounts of typing.
GALBANI for their generous supply of Italian cheeses for all my
cookery demonstrations and recipe testing.
BODUM COOKWARE for their kitchen equipment and pans used in
my work.
MAGIMIX for my cherished Gelato 2000 and Magimix 4000 food
processor.

CONTENTS

Introduction

Growing up in Italy and remembering that everything stops for the midday meal, where the streets are silent and the only sound that can be heard is of knives and forks, has made me view food – and eating – as something special.

I want my recipes to brighten the day and embrace all the senses. To me, vegetarian food shouldn't be dreary but be just as vibrant and delicious as non-vegetarian food.

'The essence of good food lies in its simplicity.' There is a very popular Italian saying: 'piu se spenne peggio se magna' – 'the more you spend the less well you eat'. This is entirely how I feel about cooking and eating, and this is what **Real Fast Vegetarian Food** is all about. It's about good simple ingredients, simply prepared and lovingly cooked to produce a totally memorable meal that hasn't taken all day.

If the ingredients are good, they shouldn't take long to cook. They should only need straightforward preparation to preserve the natural goodness and flavour. The use of good quality extra virgin olive oil is particularly important. Most of the recipes can be made within **30-40** minutes but you have to be organised as often the recipe can be prepared in stages in advance.

Above all, it's about taking the fear out of cooking. The recipes are aimed at all levels of cook, not just experienced cooks. I aim for the experienced cooks to enhance their repertoire, and to de-mystify the art of cooking for the inexperienced. The whole experience should be fun with a great result; everyone can have their own method of achieving a wonderful dish.

The choice of recipes obviously reflects my love of Italian cooking but I have also drawn on the flavours and recipes from other areas, namely Spain, France, Greece and North Africa. My food is not brown, heavy, boring food – it's just good food without meat.

I hope you will want to rush into the kitchen and start cooking!

Ursula Ferrigno

Cookery Notes

- For all the recipes, quantities are given in metric and imperial. Follow one set of measures but not a mixture as they are not interchangeable.
- A standard spoon measurement is used in all the recipes:
    1 teaspoon = one 5ml spoon
    1 tablespoon = one 15ml spoon
- All spoon measures are level.
- All eggs are medium unless otherwise stated
- Use granulated sugar, white or brown, unless otherwise stated.
- Use white or brown breadcrumbs unless otherwise stated.

The Store Cupboard

The store cupboard is designed so that at a moment's notice you can always have a delicious meal at hand. It will prevent countless journeys to the shops which can be so annoying, especially when you are in the middle of cooking.

THE STORE CUPBOARD

Here is a list of some essentials that I think the store cupboard should contain.

Pasta
Tagliatelle for rich creamy sauces; spaghetti for the most popular dishes; farfalle for the children's favourite choice; pastina for a quick broth, popular with children and older people; orecchiette for vegetable sauces.

Grains
Arborio rice for risottos – a definite must; barley for casseroles; 'OO' grade Italian flour for pasta, pastry and cakes; 'O' grade Italian flour for pizza; polenta – the coarse-grain cornmeal not the instant variety; oats for porridge; strong unbleached flour for bread making; plain flour for pastry; self raising flour for cakes.

Pulses
Although I prefer dried pulses, particularly chick-peas, cannellini and borlotti, I realise that it is not always possible to soak them overnight, boil and cook, so canned pulses are a good standby item.

Nuts and Seeds
Almonds (whole and ground) – a really useful ingredient; hazelnuts; pinenuts; pumpkin seeds; sesame seeds; sunflower seeds.

Oils
Extra virgin olive oil for dressings; olive oils for cooking.
   I'm not wildly keen on hazelnut or walnut oils but they are useful for salad dressings. Do use different oils in your cooking and experiment with them because they will improve and enhance your dishes no end.

Dried Fruits
If possible choose those not preserved with sulphur dioxide as they have more flavour and nutritional value.
Apricots; prunes; figs; pears; apples raisins; sultanas.

Herbs and Spices
Sea salt (coarse and flake varieties); black peppercorns – whole to freshly grind yourself; wholegrain mustard; bay leaves; rosemary; thyme; fennel seeds; saffron; nutmeg (whole to grate as you need); marjoram.

Miscellaneous
Sugar; cans of tomatoes; concentrated tomato paste.

Cheeses
Although perishable and should therefore be stored in the fridge, cheeses usually have a good shelf life.

Cheeses are usually made with animal rennet and therefore not suitable for the strict vegetarian. However the range of cheeses available made with vegetable rennet – including Parmesan – is increasing, so look out for them if this is important to you.

Suggested cheeses include mature Cheddar, goats' cheese and a hard Italian cheese such as Parmesan, Pecorino and Grana Padano.

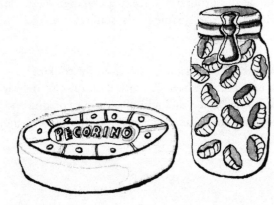

Breakfasts and Brunches

Breakfasts are vital to help sustain energy levels through a long and often busy day. With good food inside you from the outset, not only will your performance be improved but you will feel happier and healthier. I know myself how terrible I look and feel if I've skipped breakfast. Breakfasts kick-start your body into action and help to keep you alert and creative. Lack of time is no excuse for, in this chapter, I've included some recipes which don't take long to prepare. There are also recipes for brunches for those who like to rise late and enjoy a leisurely start to the day.

MANGO AND BANANA SHAKE

This recipe is a variation on a theme. I first enjoyed it on a skiing trip to Val d'Isere. It was the first time I had ever had soya milk and I must say I was pleasantly surprised. Soya milk is very light, nutritious and easy to digest. On its own it's less appealing but blended with fruits and honey it's delicious and definitely makes a great store cupboard standby.

SERVES 2

1 mango
1 banana
300ml (10fl oz) soya milk
3-4 teaspoons runny honey
pinch of ground cinnamon

grated rind of 1 unwaxed lemon
handful of raisins
general pinch of sesame seeds
6 ice cubes

- Stand the mango on a board on its long, rounded edge. Cut a thick slice down either side of the mango, keeping the knife as close to the stone as possible. Scrape the mango flesh out of the skin. Peel the banana.

- Put the fruits and remaining ingredients in a food processor or blender and blend until smooth, thick and creamy.

- Pour into glasses and serve immediately.

HERBED OMELETTE SANDWICH

This breakfast idea was borne out of a craving for something tasty, nutritious and quick, yet something that I could eat on a long car journey (I have a lot of these travelling to cookery demonstrations). It can equally be eaten at home and makes a great late-rising bridge between breakfast and lunch.

SERVES 4

4 large free range eggs
handful of snipped chives
6-8 sprigs of flat-leaved fresh
    parsley, finely chopped
salt and pepper
1 tablespoon milk or water

6 spring onions
2 tablespoons olive oil
8 slices of open-textured bread,
    toasted
handful of chopped fresh rocket

- Beat the eggs in a medium bowl. Add the chives, parsley, salt, pepper, milk or water. Finely chop the spring onions, add to the mixture and beat well.

- Heat the oil in a medium frying pan, add the egg mixture and whisk in the centre until the omelette just begins to set. Lower the heat and leave until golden underneath.

- Pre-heat the grill and cook the omelette under the grill until brown on top.

- Cut the omelette into quarters and place between the toast. Serve sprinkled with rocket.

ROASTED CHERRY TOMATOES ON TOAST

Cherry tomatoes have a good flavour throughout the year and tend to be sweet and not nearly as disappointing as other varieties. I try to buy vine cherry tomatoes and those that have been grown in a sunny climate. Smell the stalk end too – it should smell peppery. This breakfast idea is for the weekend and can double up for an easy lunch.

SERVES 4

500g (1lb) cherry tomatoes
a little olive oil
sprig of fresh rosemary
4 thick slices of ciabatta bread, cut in half

a little extra virgin olive oil
salt and pepper
shavings of Parmesan cheese
handful of torn fresh basil

- Pre-heat the oven to 200°C, 400°F, Gas Mark 6.

- Place the tomatoes on a baking tray, drizzle with olive oil and scatter over some fresh rosemary leaves. Bake for 12 minutes until soft, squashy and slightly golden.

- Toast the ciabatta bread then brush with extra virgin olive oil. Put the tomatoes, salt, pepper, Parmesan cheese and basil in a large bowl. Using your hands, mix well together to coat the tomatoes amply with the seasonings. Put the warm tomatoes on top of the toast and serve immediately.

TROPICAL FRUIT AND YOGURT SHAKE

Light and refreshing, this drink is packed with Vitamin C. It is one of my favourite combinations. I hope you will enjoy it too. For texture, you could add a handful of hazelnuts or sunflower seeds. It will keep in the fridge for up to two days.

SERVES 4

4 kiwi fruit	450ml (15fl oz) natural yogurt
2 oranges	150ml (5fl oz) apple juice
1 banana	

- Peel and roughly chop the kiwi fruit. Peel the oranges and banana.

- Put the fruits, yogurt and apple juice in a food processor and blend until smooth. Serve chilled.

SCRAMBLED EGGS WITH CHEESE ON A BAGEL

My youngest sister Andrea suggested this breakfast. She and her husband and baby Matthew all enjoy it at least three times a week. Andrea suggested the Gruyère cheese on the top because of its nutty flavour and she uses single cream when she wants to add a touch of luxury.

SERVES 4

4 free range eggs	25g (1oz) unsalted butter
150ml (¼ pint) milk or single cream	4 bagels
salt and pepper	100g (4oz) Gruyère cheese

- Break the eggs into a medium bowl and add the milk or cream, salt and pepper. Mix together well.

- In a medium frying pan, melt the butter over a moderate heat. Add the egg mixture and keep stirring, with a wooden spoon, until the eggs start to cook and then scramble.

- Toast the bagels and grate the cheese. Serve the eggs on the top of a bagel with the cheese sprinkled on top. Serve immediately.

FRENCH TOAST

Some people like to serve this toast smothered in sugar once it is cooked.
My sisters and I were never allowed to.

SERVES 4

3 free range eggs
4 slices of medium sliced bread

2-3 tablespoons olive oil
caster sugar, to serve (optional)

- Beat the eggs in a large, shallow dish. Immerse the bread slices in the egg and leave for 5-7 minutes.

- Heat the oil in a large frying pan. Add the bread slices and fry for 6 minutes, on each side, until golden. Sprinkle with caster sugar if wished and serve immediately.

SAUTE POTATOES WITH MUSHROOMS AND ROSEMARY

This is ideal to serve when you are making a late start at the weekend. Please do use really fresh mushrooms to enjoy this dish at its best.

SERVES 4

450g (1lb) new potatoes
salt and pepper
1 onion
4 tablespoons olive oil

450g (1lb) flat mushrooms
2 sprigs of finely chopped rosemary
handful of fresh parsley, chopped

- Scrub the potatoes well, leaving the skin on. Cook in boiling salted water for 10-12 minutes until just tender.

- Meanwhile, slice the onion into rings. Heat 2 tablespoons of the oil in a frying pan, add the onion rings and fry for about 5 minutes until softened.

- Wipe then halve the mushrooms. In a separate pan, heat the remaining 2 tablespoons of oil, add the mushrooms and fry for 3-4 minutes until softened. Season well with salt and pepper and add the rosemary and parsley.

- Drain the cooked potatoes. Add to the mushrooms with the onion and mix together. Serve immediately.

FIGS SOAKED IN FRESH ORANGE JUICE

Dried figs are a wonderful store house of energy and rich in nutrients, particularly calcium and iron. Soaked in freshly squeezed orange juice, the figs become plump and can't be bettered. They are a great way to start the day. Serve with a generous helping of Greek yogurt. I would recommend soaking a large amount of figs at one go so that they can be enjoyed throughout the week.

SERVES 4

4 thin skinned oranges
200g (7oz) dried figs (Turkish ones
  are good)

sunflower or sesame seeds, to serve
  (optional)
Greek yogurt, to serve

- Remove the zest from 2 of the oranges and squeeze the juice from all of the oranges.

- Put the figs in a medium bowl, add the zest and pour over the orange juice. Top with water so that the figs are covered in juice.

- Cover the bowl with a plate and leave to soak overnight in the fridge. The figs will swell and plump up as they absorb the juice.

- To serve, sprinkle the seeds over the figs and top with yogurt.

HOT CRUNCHY CINNAMON TOAST

This recipe has been taken from my first book The 90's Vegetarian. *Many people who have bought the book have commented on this recipe, saying that it is a real winner. It's rather decadent but you must try it.*

SERVES 2-3

three 2cm (¾ inch) slices of white bread
40g (1½oz) unsalted butter

2 teaspoons ground cinnamon
40g (1½oz) demerara sugar

- Pre-heat the oven to 190°C, 375°F, Gas Mark 5. Lightly butter a baking tray.

- Cut the crusts off the bread and cut each slice into four strips. Melt the butter. In a bowl, stir together the cinnamon and sugar.

- Working with a strip of bread at a time, turn the strips quickly in the butter, coating them on all sides and letting any excess drip off. Turn them quickly in the cinnamon sugar, coating on all sides.

- Place the strips on the baking tray and bake for 10 minutes. Turn and bake for a further 10 minutes. Serve warm.

SPICED HOT APPLE JUICE

For a healthy start in the morning, this drink is warming and comforting. It reminds me of a non-alcoholic gluhwein.

SERVES 4

8 whole cloves
1 unwaxed lemon
3 tablespoons apple juice
concentrate (available from
health food stores)
1 cinnamon stick
3 green cardamoms

- Stick the cloves in the lemon.

- Put 600ml (1 pint) water in a saucepan and add the lemon, apple juice, cinnamon stick and cardamoms. Bring to the boil, cover and simmer for 15 minutes.

- Strain the juice and serve hot.

CHEESE AND PEPPER OMELETTE

I serve this for a weekend brunch as it is tasty and quick to make.

SERVES 4

1 small red pepper
100g (4oz) Gruyère cheese
5 free range eggs
salt and pepper

50g (2oz) freshly grated Parmesan
  cheese
1 tablespoon olive oil

- Cut the pepper into quarters then finely dice the flesh, discarding the core and seeds. Grate the Gruyère cheese.

- Lightly beat the eggs with the salt and pepper. Stir in the Gruyère and Parmesan cheese.

- In a medium frying pan, heat the oil then pour in the egg mixture. Beat the mixture again then leave to cook until the mixture has nearly set but still moist on the top. Sprinkle the red pepper over the top.

- Put the pan under a hot grill and cook for 2-3 minutes until set. Serve hot.

FRIED MOZZARELLA SANDWICHES

These really are easy to make and are such a tasty brunch dish. Use good quality mozzarella to ensure maximum flavour and season it well to bring out its subtle flavour.

SERVES 4–6

500g (1lb) Italian mozzarella cheese
salt and pepper
8 slices of white bread, crusts removed

generous handful of fresh basil
2 large free range eggs
175ml (6ft oz) milk
75g (3oz) plain flour
olive oil, for frying

- Slice the cheese thinly and season well on both sides with salt and pepper. Arrange on 4 slices of bread, leaving a generous margin around the edges. Sprinkle basil over the cheese, cover with the remaining bread slices, then cut each sandwich in half.

- Beat the eggs in a bowl and add the milk, salt and pepper. Spread flour on a flat plate.

- Brush a little egg and milk mixture inside the edges of the sandwich and press together.

- Quickly dip each sandwich into the egg mixture, then coat lightly with the flour. Dip again into the egg mixture, shaking off any excess.

- Pour enough oil into a frying pan to come 1cm (½ inch) up the sides of the pan and heat until hot. Carefully place the sandwiches in a single layer in the pan. If your pan is not big enough, cook in batches. Fry for 3 minutes on each side until brown. Drain on absorbent paper and serve hot.

Soups, Starters and Snacks

For this chapter I've collected dishes that are light, tasty and nutritious, designed for busy lives on the move. They can be made with ease and are my collection of all-time favourites. It includes warming soups which, served with crusty bread, make a good starter or a nourishing snack. The recipes for starters also double up as snacks, and then there are snacks in their own right. Many of these are also great for picnics and long car journeys and, if served with perhaps a salad, make a nutritious and more substantial meal.

ONION SOUP

This is a classic soup and such a comforting soup, too. It is ideal for a chilly winter lunch or evening meal. Use good firm French onions for a really true flavour.

SERVES 4

5 onions
50g (2oz) unsalted butter
5 tablespoons dry white wine
3 tablespoons chopped fresh thyme
1.1 litres (2 pints) vegetable stock

(see page 209)
½ a French bread
150g (5oz) Gruyère cheese
salt and pepper

- Skin the onions and chop finely. Melt the butter in a large saucepan, add the onions and fry for 5-10 minutes until golden.

- Add the wine, thyme, salt, pepper and stock and simmer for 20 minutes until golden.

- Meanwhile, cut the bread into 1cm (½ inch) thick slices and toast lightly on both sides.

- Grate the cheese. Sprinkle on top of the bread then grill until lightly brown.

- To serve, pour the soup into warmed bowls and float the cheese toasts on top.

ITALIAN TOMATO SOUP

This soup has such a fresh flavour and is made in no time. My advice to the cook is to use a good vegetable stock, preferably home-made. The breadcrumbs thicken the soup beautifully and the basil adds the perfect finishing touch.

SERVES 4-5

two 400g cans tomatoes or 700g
   (1½lb) fresh ripe tomatoes
1 onion
2 garlic cloves
2 tablespoons olive oil
750ml (1¼ pints) vegetable stock
   (see page 209)
1 tablespoon tomato purée

50g (2oz) day-old wholewheat
   breadcrumbs
handful of fresh basil leaves,
   roughly torn
salt and pepper
plenty of fresh basil leaves, to
   garnish
extra virgin olive oil, to garnish

- If using fresh tomatoes, put in a bowl, cover with boiling water for about 30 seconds then plunge into cold water. Using a sharp knife, peel off the skins then roughly chop the flesh, discarding the seeds.

- Roughly chop the onion. Crush the garlic.

- Heat the oil in a saucepan, add the onion and garlic and fry, over a moderate heat, for about 4 minutes until they begin to brown.

- Add the tomatoes, stock, tomato purée, breadcrumbs, basil leaves, salt and pepper. Bring to the boil, then lower the heat and simmer for 20 minutes.

- Serve hot, garnished with basil leaves and a little extra virgin olive oil drizzled on top.

FENNEL SOUP

Anybody familiar with my teaching courses in 'Books for Cooks' or in Italy will know of my love for fennel. Traditionally, in the South of Italy, it is cut into strips and eaten raw at the end of a meal, as a digestive because of its alkaline qualities. This soup is a particular favourite of mine as it's so light and digestible.

SERVES 6

4 medium fennel heads
1½ garlic cloves
4 tablespoons olive oil
generous handful of flat-leaved fresh parsley, chopped
1.1 litres (2 pints) hot vegetable

stock (see page 209)
salt and pepper
4 tablespoons double cream
6 sprigs of flat-leaved fresh parsley, to garnish
crusty bread, to serve

- Trim the fennel and wash well then chop finely. Crush the garlic.

- Heat the oil in a saucepan, add the garlic and fennel and fry gently for 2-3 minutes. Add the parsley, vegetable stock, salt and pepper, bring to the boil and simmer for 20 minutes.

- Purée the soup in a food processor or blender with the cream.

- Adjust seasonings, then serve garnished with a sprig of parsley and accompany with crusty bread.

STUFFED LETTUCE SOUP

This soup is very tasty and satisfying. It is also very unusual and is guaranteed to become a favourite. I first enjoyed it in Genoa on a cold day after a visit to the local market. It was most welcome and I enjoyed the unusual combination of lettuce and mushrooms with ricotta. It is a local dish served in the winter.

SERVES 4

400g (14oz) flat mushrooms
2 garlic cloves
2 tablespoons olive oil plus a little for brushing
3 tablespoons chopped fresh marjoram
200g (7oz) ricotta
2 free range eggs

2-3 tablespoons freshly grated Parmesan cheese
salt and pepper
1 large iceberg or romaine lettuce
1 litre (1¾ pints) vegetable stock (see page 209)
4 slices of coarse textured bread

- Finely chop the mushrooms. Crush the garlic.

- Heat the oil in a frying pan, add the mushrooms and fry for 2-3 minutes until softened. Add the garlic and marjoram and fry for a further 2 minutes. Remove from heat.

- Mash the ricotta with the eggs. Add the mushrooms, Parmesan cheese, salt and pepper and mix well.

- Discard the outer leaves of the lettuce and separate the rest. Blanch them in boiling water for a few seconds until they soften, then drain.

- Open each lettuce leaf carefully and place a heaped tablespoon of filling at one end.

- Roll up each leaf towards the end where the rib is thickest, tucking in the sides before the roll is finished, so that the filling does not fall out. Pack the rolls into a wide saucepan.

- Bring the stock to the boil, pour over the rolls and simmer for 2-3 minutes.

- Meanwhile, toast the bread and brush with oil.

- To serve, place the toasted bread in the bottom of the soup bowls. Put the lettuce rolls on the toast and pour over the soup.

LITTLE BREAD DUMPLINGS IN BROTH

I first enjoyed this delicious soup at lunch before my friend Christiana married. It was prepared by her Grandmother, Madellena Chapello, a great friend of mine and my Father's. This recipe calls for good stock which is included in the glossary.

SERVES 4

50g (2oz) fresh breadcrumbs
50g (2oz) freshly grated Parmesan
   cheese plus extra to serve
freshly grated nutmeg, to taste
salt and pepper

1 large free range egg
900ml (1½ pints) vegetable stock
   (see page 209)
handful of chopped flat-leaved fresh
   parsley

- To prepare the dumplings, on a large board, mix together the breadcrumbs, the Parmesan cheese, nutmeg, salt and pepper. Make a well in the centre, add the egg and knead well together for about 3 minutes.

- Pour the stock into a large saucepan, add the parsley and bring to a slow boil.

- When the stock reaches boiling point, form the dumpling mixture into tiny balls, the size of a one penny piece, and add to the stock. Boil gently for 2 minutes, remove from the heat and leave for a further 2 minutes.

- Serve with freshly grated Parmesan cheese.

DILL SOUP

Dill is an underrated herb yet this soup is delicate and delicious.

SERVES 4

2 carrots
2 celery sticks
1 onion
1 garlic clove
2 tablespoons olive oil
1 litre (1¾ pints) vegetable stock

(see page 209)
150ml (¼ pint) soured cream
6 tablespoons chopped fresh dill
salt and pepper
crusty bread, to serve

- Roughly chop the carrots and celery. Finely chop the onion and garlic.

- Heat the oil in a saucepan, add the onion and fry for 2-3 minutes. Add the carrots, celery and garlic, cover and cook gently for 10 minutes until softened.

- Allow to cool slightly then put in a food processor and blend until smooth.

- Return the mixture to the saucepan, add the stock and simmer for 10 minutes.

- Stir in the soured cream, dill, salt and pepper. Serve immediately with warm crusty bread.

FRESH PEA SOUP

I first enjoyed this soup whilst in Venice with my mother. Venice was bitterly cold, so much so that the canals were semi frozen. This soup was very welcoming.

SERVES 4

1 onion
handful of flat-leaved fresh parsley
25g (1oz) unsalted butter
225g (8oz) shelled fresh peas
1 litre (1¾ pints) vegetable stock (see page 209)

300g (11oz) arborio (risotto) rice
salt and pepper
50g (2oz) freshly grated Parmesan cheese
2-3 tablespoons extra virgin olive oil

- Finely chop the onion and parsley. Melt the butter in a large frying pan. Add the onion and fry for 5 minutes until lightly coloured.

- Add the peas and 2-3 tablespoons of stock. Cover and simmer for 10 minutes.

- Add the rice and remaining stock and bring to the boil. Lower the heat, cover and simmer for 20 minutes until the rice is tender.

- Season with salt and pepper, add the Parmesan cheese and sprinkle over the parsley. Remove from the heat and leave to stand for 1 minute before serving.

- To serve, drizzle over the olive oil to add more flavour.

ROASTED TOMATO AND GARLIC SOUP

I love this recipe, it's an all-time favourite. Roasting the tomatoes before making the soup intensifies their flavour and although it has a whole garlic head in it, you will be surprised how sweet and mild it becomes. Although this soup takes longer than 30 minutes to make, most of this time is taken up with cooking. I recommend that you make double quantities for it tastes even better the next day.

SERVES 4

1kg (2lb) small ripe tomatoes	2 parsley stalks
olive oil	salt and pepper
1 whole garlic head	4 tablespoons crème fraîche or
2 onions	soured cream
2 carrots	crusty bread, to serve
2 celery sticks	

- Pre-heat the oven to 200°C, 400°F, Gas Mark 6.

- Remove the stems from the tomatoes and place in a roasting dish, in a single layer. Drizzle with a little olive oil and roast in the oven for 20-30 minutes, depending on their size, until they begin to colour and split.

- Meanwhile, break up the garlic head and place the unpeeled cloves in a small ovenproof dish. Drizzle with a little olive oil and roast for 15 minutes or until they are very soft.

- Squeeze the soft cloves out of their papery skins.

- Skin and roughly chop the onions. Peel and slice the carrots. Slice the celery sticks. Heat 3 tablespoons olive oil in a saucepan. Add the onion, carrot and celery and fry for 10 minutes until soft.

- Add the roasted garlic cloves, the tomatoes with their juice, 600ml (1 pint) water, the parsley stalks and salt and pepper to taste. Bring to the boil then simmer for 20 minutes. Remove the parsley stalks.

- Purée the soup in a food processor or blender.

- Adjust the seasoning and serve hot, with a swirl of crème fraîche in each bowl. Accompany with crusty bread.

SKEWERS OF TOASTED BREAD WITH PEPPERS AND MOZZARELLA CHEESE

This is such a simple starter yet looks elegant and attractive. It is also colourful and reminds me of the Italian flag – red, white and green.

SERVES 4

2 large red peppers	3 tablespoons olive oil
1 French bread	salt and pepper
3 medium mozzarella cheeses	50g (2oz) unsalted butter
2 handfuls of fresh basil leaves	sprigs of flat-leaved fresh parsley

- Pre-heat the oven to 200°C, 400°F, Gas Mark 6.

- Place the peppers on a baking tray and roast in the oven for 20 minutes until deflated and slightly charred. Leave to cool, then peel off the skin. Cut the flesh of each into 12 pieces, discarding the core and seeds.

- Cut the bread into 20 slices. Cut the mozzarella cheeses into 1cm (½ inch) thick slices, making a total of 16 slices.

- Thread 4 skewers, allowing 5 slices of bread per skewer. Start with the bread and alternate with the red pepper pieces, cheese and basil leaves. Place the skewers on an oiled baking tray.

- Brush the skewers with the oil and season with salt and pepper.

- Bake in the oven for 8 minutes, turning after 4 minutes and checking to see that the skewers don't burn.

- Melt the butter and pour over the skewers. Serve garnished with a sprig of parsley.

STUFFED MUSHROOMS

Tasty and simple, this is one of Italy's classics. In Portobello Road Market there is a stall that always has fantastic organic mushrooms. This dish lends itself to the best mushrooms you can find, fresh and full of flavour. You can experiment with this dish and add different herbs such as marjoram and sage. It makes a great starter or snack.

SERVES 6

2 tablespoons milk
2 slices of bread, crusts removed
6 large flat mushrooms
4-6 tablespoons olive oil
salt and pepper
large bunch of flat-leaved fresh
parsley
2 garlic cloves
50g (2oz) freshly grated Parmesan cheese
2-3 tablespoons brandy (optional)

- Pour the milk over the bread and leave to soak. Wipe the mushrooms and remove and reserve the stalks.

- In a large frying pan, heat 2-3 tablespoons olive oil. Add the mushrooms and fry for 5 minutes or until just tender, sprinkling with salt and pepper and turning them over once.

- Arrange the mushrooms, stem side up, in a flameproof dish. Squeeze the milk out of the bread.

- For the stuffing, put the reserved mushroom stalks and parsley in a food processor and chop finely. Add the soaked bread and process a little longer.

- Turn the mixture into a bowl. Crush the garlic and add with the Parmesan cheese and a little salt and pepper. Moisten with brandy to taste and 2-3 tablespoons olive oil and mix well together.

- Preheat the grill. Press a little stuffing into each mushroom cap and grill for about 5 minutes until golden. Serve hot.

CROSTINI WITH AUBERGINE PUREE

*I first enjoyed these crostini while teaching in Umbria. As is the custom
there, the waiter arrived and, having supplied us with wine, water
and bread, proceeded to tell us what we were going to eat. There was no
menu, instead we listened as he reeled off a list of delicious sounding
dishes. I sometimes worry that the food may not live up to the
description, but as soon as these crostini arrived, I knew we were on to a
good thing. So much so that I asked the chef for the recipe.*

SERVES 4

1 French bread
olive oil
2 medium aubergines
½ garlic clove
2 tablespoons extra virgin olive oil
2 teaspoons Greek yogurt

juice of ½ lemon
1 tablespoon chopped fresh parsley
   (optional)
salt and pepper
4 halves of sun-dried tomatoes
fresh coriander leaves, to garnish

- Pre-heat the oven to 180°C, 350°F, Gas Mark 4.

- To prepare the crostini, thinly slice the French bread then brush both
  sides with olive oil. Place the slices of bread on baking trays and bake
  in the oven for 10-12 minutes until brown. Leave to cool on a wire
  rack.

- To prepare the aubergine purée, pre-heat the oven to 200°C,
  400°F, Gas Mark 6. Place the aubergines on a rack, standing in a
  roasting tin, and bake in the oven for 25-30 minutes until the skins
  are wrinkled and charred.

- Remove the skin from the aubergines, place the flesh in a sieve and
  press out all the juices.

- Put the aubergine flesh and the garlic in a food processor and blend to form a purée. Gradually add the virgin olive oil in a thin stream. Mix in the yogurt, lemon juice and parsley and season well with salt and pepper.

- Cut the sun-dried tomatoes into strips. To serve, spread the crostini with generous mounds of the aubergine purée, lay a strip of sun-dried tomato on each and garnish with a coriander leaf.

GREEN OLIVE PASTE

This is a mixture of typical Spanish produce which can be used as a spread to serve as a tapas. It is an ideal snack to hand around to guests when you are having a barbecue or party. It's totally straightforward to make and can be kept in the fridge in a jar with a film of olive oil on the top. This will act as a preservative and, providing it always has a film of oil, will last indefinitely. I therefore suggest that you make a large batch.

SERVES 4

40 stoned green olives
1 teaspoon capers
1 tablespoon ground almonds
1 garlic clove
4 tablespoons olive oil

¼ teaspoon ground cumin
¼ teaspoon ground paprika
12 slices of French bread, to serve
pimientos or flat-leaved parsley
    leaves, to garnish

- Place all the ingredients, except the bread and pimiento, in a food processor and blend to form purée.

- To serve, spread thinly on the slices of bread and garnish with pieces of pimiento or parsley.

GORGONZOLA BRUSCHETTA WITH CHERRY TOMATOES

Blue cheese is particularly good for you because of the natural penicillin present, so, if you're feeling run down, don't rush to the medicine cabinet but try this recipe instead!

SERVES 4

2-3 tablespoons olive oil	salt and pepper
4 slices of open-textured bread	175g (6oz) Gorgonzola cheese
1 garlic clove	4 large basil leaves
8 cherry tomatoes	

- Pre-heat oven to 200°C, 400°F, Gas Mark 6.

- Brush the oil on both sides of the bread and place on a baking tray. Bake in the oven for 10 minutes until golden. Rub the bread with the garlic.

- Halve the cherry tomatoes, sprinkle with salt and pepper and place on a baking tray. Bake in the oven for 10 minutes until lightly browned and slightly squashy. Meanwhile, slice the cheese.

- Now assemble the bruschetta whilst the bread and tomatoes are still warm. First place slices of cheese on the bread slices, then basil leaves and finally the tomatoes. Serve warm.

NEAPOLITAN BAKED TOMATOES

This Neapolitan way of cooking tomatoes has been adopted all over Italy and I love the simplicity of this dish. Choose your tomatoes with discretion, they are so important. Smell the stalk end for a good peppery flavour, buy tomatoes from a sunny climate and choose those with a good deep red colour.

SERVES 4

4 large, ripe, firm tomatoes	salt
1 garlic clove	a few sprigs of fresh marjoram,
4 tablespoons chopped fresh parsley	chopped
4 tablespoons fresh breadcrumbs	1 tablespoon capers (optional)
4 tablespoons olive oil	

- Pre-heat the oven to 180°C, 350°F, Gas Mark 4.

- Cut the tomatoes in half. Crush the garlic.

- Mix together the garlic, parsley, breadcrumbs, oil, salt, marjoram and capers, if using.

- Place the tomatoes, cut side up, in a greased ovenproof dish. Cover them with the parsley and breadcrumb mixture and bake in the oven for 20 minutes. Turn up the oven to 190°C, 375°F, Gas Mark 5 and cook for a further 10 minutes until the topping is crisp but do not let the tomatoes get too soft. Serve hot or warm.

AUBERGINE AND CHEESE SANDWICH

I enjoyed this sandwich recently on a trip to Rome. It was so good that I just had to have another one. I have a great deal of respect for aubergines. If they have been degorged, that is the bitterness removed, they taste so much better and also absorb less oil.

SERVES 2

1 small aubergine
salt and pepper
2-3 tablespoons olive oil plus extra
    for storing the aubergine (see
    method)
a thin slice of garlic

2 small pain rustique or pieces of
    French bread
4 cos lettuce leaves
4 slices of mozzarella cheese
handful of fresh basil

- Thinly slice the aubergine lengthways. Sprinkle with salt, place in a bowl, cover and weigh down. Leave for 30 minutes.

- Rinse the aubergine slices well and pat dry. Heat the oil in a frying pan and fry the slices for 3 minutes on each side or until golden. Remove from the pan and drain on kitchen paper.

- There will be more aubergines fried than are necessary for the sandwiches, so you can place them in a container, add the garlic and enough oil to cover the aubergine. Cover and store in the fridge for up to 2 weeks.

- To assemble the sandwiches, slice the bread in half lengthways. On the base arrange the lettuce, cheese, seasoned with salt and pepper, aubergine slices and basil. Top with the bread and serve.

ROASTED SHALLOT AND MARJORAM CHEESE ON TOAST

I really enjoy the flavour of roasted shallots as they are sweet and succulent. Roasting is such an easy way to preserve all the flavour within the shallot skins and they combine wonderfully with cheese and marjoram – a herb so often neglected.

SERVES 4

250g (8oz) shallots	2 tablespoons stout
1 tablespoon olive oil	25g (1oz) unsalted butter
salt and pepper	4 tablespoons chopped fresh
100g (4oz) mature Cheddar cheese	marjoram
1 teaspoon wholegrain mustard	4 slices of bread (Granary is good)

- Pre-heat the oven to 220°C, 425°F, Gas Mark 7.

- Skin the shallots, cut in half and put in a roasting tin. Drizzle over the oil, season with salt and pepper and bake for 10 minutes until golden.

- Grate the cheese and put in a small saucepan with the mustard, stout, butter, marjoram, salt and pepper. Heat gently, stirring until creamy then add the shallots.

- Toast the bread on both sides and pour the cheese and shallot mixture on top.

- Place under the grill for 1-2 minutes until bubbling. Serve hot.

PEPPER AND OLIVE TORTILLA

This Italian recipe is wonderful when served hot with its melting cheese topping but it could equally well form part of a cold summer picnic or snack, as it does in Spain.

SERVES 4-6

1 red pepper
1 green pepper
1 yellow pepper
3 tablespoons olive oil
50g (2oz) stuffed green olives
50g (2oz) black olives

6 free range eggs
2 egg yolks
1 tablespoon chopped fresh parsley
salt and pepper
75g (3oz) Gruyère or mature
    Cheddar cheese

- Cut the peppers in half, discard the core and seeds and cut the flesh into bite size chunks.

- Heat the oil in a deep frying pan, add the peppers and fry gently for 5 minutes.

- Add the olives and continue cooking for a further 2 minutes.

- Beat the eggs and egg yolks together. Add the parsley, salt and pepper. Pour into the pan and cook over a moderate heat until nearly set.

- Meanwhile, slice the cheese then arrange the slices over the top of the eggs and place under a hot grill for 2-3 minutes until the cheese begins to melt and brown.

- Slide the tortilla on to a plate and serve cut into wedges.

ENDIVE WITH CANNELLINI BEAN PUREE

This makes an interesting snack as the endive can be eaten with the bean purée in its hollow, topped with an olive and a sprig of parsley. It is nutritious and satisfying. Endive, in fact, are an excellent stimulant for the liver. They have the most flavour during the winter months when their leaves are thicker.

SERVES 4

two 400g cans cannellini beans, drained
½ a garlic clove
2 tablespoons extra virgin olive oil
2 teaspoons marjoram
2 teaspoons lemon juice
2 endives
25g (1oz) black olives, to garnish
flat-leaved fresh parsley, to garnish

- Mash the cannellini beans. Crush the garlic then stir into the beans with the olive oil, marjoram and lemon juice.

- Wash and dry the endive leaves. Divide the endive between 4 plates and arrange the purée on the leaves.

- Serve garnished with the olives and parsley.

ROASTED RED PEPPER, CREAM CHEESE AND ROCKET OPEN SANDWICHES

The sweetness from the pepper and the pepperiness from the rocket makes this sandwich very delicious. It's colourful too. You can prepare the cheese mixture in advance for it will keep in the fridge, covered, for up to two days.

SERVES 4

1 red pepper
100g (4oz) cream cheese
salt and pepper

4 slices of bread, such as foccacia
handful of rocket

- Pre-heat the oven to 200°C, 400°F, Gas Mark 6.

- Put the pepper on a baking tray and roast in the oven for 20 minutes until deflated and slightly charred, turning once during cooking. Leave to cool, then peel off the skin.

- Chop the pepper flesh, discarding the core and seeds and put in a bowl. Add the cheese, season with salt and pepper and mix together.

- To assemble the sandwiches, spread the roasted pepper and cheese mixture generously on the slices of bread, cut each slice in half and top with rocket.

Accompanying Vegetables

The Europeans are the original market gardeners. Their land is utilised to the full. They don't have lawns and rose bushes as we do in the UK, but instead their land is used to grow vegetables. Even the Station Master has his little cultivated plot. For this reason the vegetable dishes are inventive and good. The recipes in this chapter have been collected from all over Europe and from this selection you will find a recipe to complement a main course.

GIANT STUFFED MUSHROOMS

Flat mushrooms, also known as field mushrooms, have infinitely more flavour than button mushrooms which, because they are picked so small, have not been allowed to develop their flavour. Never wash mushrooms as they become water logged, just wipe with kitchen paper to remove dirt and grit.

SERVES 6

6 large flat mushrooms
2 slices of bread, crusts removed
2 tablespoons milk
4-6 tablespoons olive oil
salt and pepper
large bunch of flat-leaved fresh

parsley
2 garlic cloves
50g (2oz) freshly grated Parmesan
   cheese
2-3 tablespoons brandy (optional)

- Wipe the mushrooms, remove the stalks and reserve. Soak the bread in the milk.

- In a large frying pan, heat 2-3 tablespoons of oil. Add the whole mushrooms and fry for 5 minutes or until just tender, sprinkling with salt and pepper and turning them over once.

- Arrange the mushrooms stem side up, side by side, in a flameproof dish.

- For the stuffing, put the mushrooms stalks and parsley in a food processor and chop finely.

- Squeeze the bread dry, add to the mushroom mixture and process a little longer. Turn the mixture into a bowl. Crush the garlic and add with the Parmesan cheese, salt and pepper. Moisten with brandy to taste and with 2-3 tablespoons olive oil and mix together.

- Pre-heat the grill. Press a little stuffing into each mushroom cap and grill for about 5 minutes until golden. Serve hot.

WHITE BEANS WITH TOMATO AND SAGE

This is one of Tuscany's most famous bean dishes. The Italian name for this dish, Fagioli all'uccelletto, *literally means 'beans like birds', supposedly because the sage, onion, garlic and tomato makes the flavour of the beans resemble that of small game birds.*

SERVES 6

50ml (2fl oz) olive oil	225g (8oz) canned tomatoes
25g (1oz) butter	two 400g cans white haricot beans,
3 garlic cloves, crushed	drained
12 fresh sage leaves	salt and pepper

- Heat the olive oil and butter in a saucepan, add the garlic and sage and fry for 1 minute.

- Add the tomatoes and cook over a moderate heat for 3 minutes. Add the beans, season with salt and pepper to taste and simmer for a further 5 minutes. Serve hot.

RATATOUILLE OF FRENCH BEANS

This is a speciality of Domiodossola in the Piedmont region of Northern Italy. It is a really tasty bean recipe, and even better made the day before as all the flavours will have mingled together. I like it as a simple meal served with crusty bread and a salad to follow.

SERVES 6

1kg (2lb) French beans
1 small onion
2 tablespoons olive oil
2 garlic cloves, crushed
2 tablespoons chopped fresh flat-
leaved parsley
handful of fresh basil leaves
50ml (2fl oz) dry red wine
225g (8oz) canned tomatoes
salt and pepper

- Top and tail the beans and cut them into 5cm (2 inch) lengths. Chop the onion.

- Heat the olive oil in a large frying pan, add the onion, garlic, parsley and basil, reserving a few leaves to garnish, and fry for 3 minutes. Add the red wine and cook over a moderate heat until the wine has almost evaporated.

- Meanwhile, chop the tomatoes, discarding the seeds. Add to the pan with the beans and season with salt and pepper to taste.

- Simmer for 30 minutes or until the beans are tender and the sauce has thickened. Serve sprinkled with some freshly torn basil leaves.

SLICES OF BAKED AUBERGINE WITH PARMESAN

Aubergines are one of my favourite vegetables – I love their versatility. I even have a delicious recipe for chocolate aubergines which was passed down to me from my Grandmother. This is a dish that can be served with crusty bread, a glass of rich red wine and a crisp green salad to follow.

SERVES 4

2 medium aubergines	3 sprigs of fresh rosemary
salt and pepper	grated rind of 1 unwaxed lemon
1 onion	handful of fresh basil leaves
125ml (4fl oz) olive oil	125g (4oz) Parmesan cheese
400g can tomatoes	shavings

- Pre-heat the oven to 200°C, 400°F, Gas Mark 6.

- Slice the aubergines into 1cm (½ inch) thick rounds. Sprinkle with salt, put in a bowl, cover and weigh down. Leave for 15 minutes to remove the aubergines' bitter juices.

- Meanwhile, make the tomato sauce. Chop the onion. Heat 2 tablespoons of the oil in a saucepan, add the onion and fry for 3 minutes until softened. Add the tomatoes, salt and pepper. Bring to the boil, cover and leave to simmer gently.

- After 15 minutes, rinse the aubergines and pat dry. Place on a greased baking tray and sprinkle over the rosemary. Bake in the oven for 10 minutes until golden.

- Add the lemon rind to the tomato sauce and mix well. Taste the sauce and adjust seasonings if necessary.

- Place a layer of aubergines in a casserole dish and sprinkle with some of the basil and the Parmesan cheese. Add a layer of tomato sauce, followed by aubergines, basil and Parmesan cheese. Continue layering in this way, finishing with Parmesan cheese on top.

- Bake in the oven for 10 minutes until bubbling. Serve hot.

FENNEL WITH CHEESE AND CREAM

*This recipe is blissfully straightforward and guaranteed to make
everyone who tries it firm fennel lovers! If you are not so keen, or
dubious about fennel, please try it. I have converted many people. Serve
with a baked potato and green salad.*

SERVES 6

1kg (2lb) fennel heads	4 tablespoons freshly grated
salt and pepper	Parmesan cheese
	300ml (½ pint) double cream

- Pre-heat the oven to 200°C, 400°F, Gas Mark 6. Generously butter an ovenproof dish.

- Remove the fennels' tough outer leaves, trim and wash well. Cut the heads into quarters and simmer in salted water for 7-8 minutes until very tender but not floppy.

- Drain well and arrange the pieces in one layer in the prepared dish. Sprinkle with Parmesan cheese and the salt and pepper then pour the cream over the top.

- Bake in the oven for 15-20 minutes until golden brown. Serve sizzling hot.

STUFFED AUBERGINES WITH ALMONDS

I think simple flavours are always the best, as illustrated in this vegetable dish. I often make it in advance as it gives the dish time for the flavours to develop. Cook just before serving.

SERVES 4-6

3 small aubergines, each weighing about 225g (8oz)
1 onion
1 garlic clove
handful of fresh parsley
3-4 plum tomatoes
50ml (2fl oz) olive oil

2 teaspoons fresh oregano
40g (1½oz) ground almonds
15g (½oz) breadcrumbs
salt and pepper
40g (1½oz) freshly grated Parmesan cheese

- Pre-heat the oven to 180°C, 350°F, Gas Mark 4.

- Put the aubergines in a saucepan of boiling water, cover and simmer for 5 minutes. Remove and cut in half lengthways. Scoop out the flesh, taking care not to damage the skins, to leave a shell 3mm (⅛ inch) thick. Roughly chop the flesh.

- Chop the onion, crush the garlic and finely chop the parsley. Put the tomatoes in a bowl, cover with boiling water for about 30 seconds then plunge into cold water. Using a sharp knife, peel off the skins then chop the flesh, discarding the seeds.

- Heat the olive oil in a frying pan, add the onion, garlic, parsley and oregano and fry over a moderate heat for 3 minutes. Add the chopped aubergine and tomatoes. Cover and simmer for 10 minutes or until the aubergine is tender.

- Remove the pan from the heat and stir in the ground almonds, breadcrumbs, salt and pepper.

- Fill the aubergine shells with the mixture and sprinkle the grated cheese on top.

- Place the aubergines side by side, in a well-greased shallow baking dish and bake in the oven for 30 minutes or until the top is browned. Serve hot or cold.

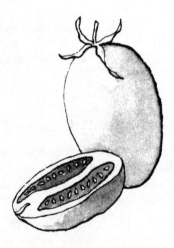

ASPARAGUS WITH CREAM SAUCE

I am always thrilled to see new season asparagus and rush out and eat it every day with all its variations. This is a classical way of enjoying asparagus and is a typical dish from Normandy. Cooking in Normandy is characterised by rich cream and excellent butter, especially that of Isigny. Rouen, also in Normandy, is known as 'The Butter Town' and people say that it was built with the dues paid to the church by the village inhabitants, so that they could eat butter during Lent.

SERVES 4

1.5kg (3¼lb) asparagus	200ml (7fl oz) double cream
salt and pepper	handful fresh chervil leaves
50g (2oz) Normandy butter	

- Tie the asparagus in bundles and stand them upright in a large saucepan of boiling salted water. Cook gently for 10-15 minutes until tender.

- Pre-heat the oven to 190°C, 375°F, Gas Mark 5. Use the butter to liberally grease a long, rectangular, ovenproof dish.

- Drain the asparagus on a clean tea-towel then arrange on the prepared dish. Season the cream with salt and pepper and pour over the asparagus.

- Bake in the oven for 10 minutes until the cream has reduced and thickened. Serve sprinkled with chervil.

CAULIFLOWER FROM AMALFI

This is a wonderful way of preparing cauliflower. You will never enjoy cauliflower cheese in quite the same way again. My tip is to cook the cauliflower with some broken bay leaves to add a subtle bay flavour and also to take away the smell that cauliflower gives when cooking.

SERVES 4

1 medium cauliflower	Parmesan cheese
2 tablespoons white unbleached plain flour	salt and pepper
2 free range eggs	3 tablespoons olive oil, for frying
4 tablespoons freshly grated	flat-leaved fresh parsley, to garnish

- Break the cauliflower into florets then steam for 6 minutes until tender. Leave to cool.

- Coat the cauliflower florets in flour, one at a time.

- Beat the eggs then add the Parmesan cheese, salt and pepper. Dip the florets in the egg mixture.

- Heat the oil in a frying pan and when hot, fry the cauliflower florets until golden and brown. Serve hot, cold or warm, scattered with parsley leaves.

GIAMBOTTA

This vegetable casserole is my Grandmother's and Mother's favourite family recipe. My Grandmother used to make four times the recipe and keep it until the next day. It never lasted a long time with my sisters and family around!

SERVES 4

1 small aubergine	2 red peppers
salt and pepper	3 teaspoons fennel seeds
1 medium onion	2-3 tablespoons olive oil
1 garlic clove	400 g can tomatoes
1 potato	6 tablespoons red wine
1 courgette	

- Cut the aubergine into cubes. Sprinkle with salt, place in a bowl, cover and weigh down. Leave for 15 minutes.

- Meanwhile, chop the onion and crush the garlic. Cut the potato and courgette into chunks. Cut the peppers in half, discarding the core and seeds then cut the flesh into chunks. Crush the fennel seeds.

- Heat the oil in a saucepan, add the onion and garlic and fry for 5 minutes until lightly browned.

- Rinse the aubergine cubes and pat dry. Add to the pan with all the remaining ingredients.

- Simmer gently for 25-30 minutes, until the vegetables are tender, adding a little water if necessary. Serve hot.

ARTICHOKE HEARTS WITH ALMOND SAUCE

This does sound like a strange combination but really it is excellent. The almonds produce a creamy sauce which can also be served with other vegetables, such as potatoes or cauliflower.

SERVES 4

½ onion
1 garlic clove
5 tablespoons olive oil
100g (4oz) ground almonds
300ml (10fl oz) vegetable stock (see page 209)
1 tablespoon cider vinegar

1 teaspoon sugar
juice of 1 lemon
salt and pepper
8 artichoke hearts (canned or bottled)
2 tablespoons capers (optional)

- Finely chop the onion. Crush the garlic. Heat 1 tablespoon oil in a saucepan, add the onion and garlic and fry for 2-3 minutes.

- Add the almonds, pour in the stock and simmer for about 15 minutes until thick and creamy.

- Beat in the remaining 4 tablespoons oil, the vinegar, sugar, lemon juice and salt and pepper.

- Arrange the artichoke hearts on individual plates. Chop the capers if using. Pour the sauce over the artichokes and garnish with the capers. Serve cold.

BAKED BEETS WITH NUT AND CHEESE CRUMB

This recipe is taken from my first book, The 90's Vegetarian. *I enjoy beetroots and think that they are vastly underrated. These vegetables are delicious and nutritious.*

SERVES 4

6 medium fresh beetroots	3 tablespoons olive oil
75g (3oz) whole almonds	100g (4oz) fresh breadcrumbs
75g (3oz) any variety of mature, hard cheese	salt and pepper

- Pre-heat the oven to 180°C, 350°F, Gas Mark 4.

- Wash the beetroots very well to remove all the soil and grime. Put in an ovenproof dish and bake in their skins for 30 minutes.

- Meanwhile, toast the nuts on a sheet of foil under the grill, turning them frequently. Put in a food processor and blend until finely ground.

- Grate the cheese. Mix the nuts, cheese, olive oil, breadcrumbs and salt and pepper together in bowl.

- Slip the skins off the beetroots and cut into 5mm (¼ inch) thick slices.

- Arrange the beetroot slices in a shallow ovenproof dish and top with the breadcrumb mixture.

- Bake in the oven at 200°C, 400°F, Gas Mark 6 for 10 minutes until golden. Serve hot or cold.

TOMATO GRATIN

There are so many recipes for baked tomatoes. This one, from Provence, is good because it is so simple.

SERVES 8

4 large ripe beef tomatoes
salt and pepper
4 garlic cloves
large bunch of flat-leaved parsley
1 tablespoon chopped fresh

rosemary leaves
40g (1½oz) breadcrumbs
3 tablespoons freshly grated
Parmesan cheese
75ml (3fl oz) olive oil

- Pre-heat the oven to 190°C, 375°F, Gas Mark 5. Grease a shallow, ovenproof dish.

- Cut the tomatoes in half and sprinkle lightly with salt. Put them, cut side up, in the prepared dish.

- Crush the garlic and finely chop the parsley. Mix together the garlic, parsley, rosemary, breadcrumbs, cheese, oil and pepper then press some of the mixture on top of each tomato half.

- Bake in the oven for 20 minutes or until the tomatoes are soft but still hold their shape. Serve hot.

SALSA DE MOJO

This is a piquant sauce, unique to the Canary Islands, which has a wonderful rich scent and taste. It is usually served with potatoes boiled in their skins or other seasonal vegetables. I find it particularly good poured over freshly steamed celeriac.

SERVES 4

2-3 large garlic cloves
1 teaspoon cumin seeds
1 teaspoon paprika
3-4 teaspoons fresh thyme
50ml (2fl oz) extra virgin olive oil

2 teaspoons wine vinegar
50ml (2fl oz) warm water
500g (1lb) seasonal vegetables of
   your choice

- In a mortar or food processor, crush together the garlic and cumin seeds until ground very finely.

- Add the paprika and thyme then add the olive oil, a drop at a time, until well mixed. Add the vinegar, then the water. Leave to cool.

- Cook the vegetables of your choice and serve with the sauce.

TIAN OF BAKED COURGETTES

Provençal dishes take their name from the local earthenware casserole, the tian, in which they are cooked. This particular one, provided by Martine Bourdon-Williams of Nice, is a pleasant mixture of different textures and flavours. Make a large amount because you will enjoy it and eat more than you think. I always make this dish when I'm entertaining a large group of students.

SERVES 8

1.5kg (3lb) tender young
  courgettes
salt and pepper
225g (8 oz) short grain rice
2 large onions
1 garlic clove
3 tablespoons olive oil

225g (8oz) fresh tender-leaf
  spinach
large bunch of fresh parsley
3 free range eggs
handful of torn fresh basil leaves
100g (4oz) freshly grated Parmesan
  cheese

- Trim the courgettes but leave them whole and unpeeled. Boil in salted water for 10 minutes or steam until tender.

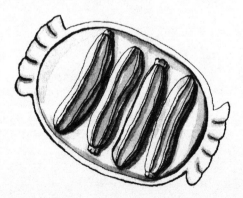

- Cook the rice in boiling salted water for 10 minutes.

- Meanwhile, finely chop the onions and garlic. Heat 2 tablespoons of the oil in a frying pan. Add the onion and garlic and fry for 5 minutes until golden.

- Pre-heat the oven to 200°C, 400°F, Gas Mark 6. Grease a large ovenproof dish with the remaining oil.

- Turn the cooked courgettes into a colander and mash with a potato masher, letting the juices drain away.

- Finely shred the spinach. Finely chop the parsley. In a large bowl, lightly beat the eggs and add the spinach, parsley, basil, Parmesan cheese and pepper, then add the mashed courgettes, the fried garlic and onion and the rice. Mix well together and taste before adding any salt.

- Pour the mixture into the prepared dish and bake in the oven for 30 minutes or until firm and browned on top. Serve hot.

BROAD BEANS WITH FRESH CHEESE

In Italy, when broad beans have just come into season and they are very young and tender, they are eaten raw with their pods and skins removed. The locals sit eating the beans 'passa tempo' to pass the time with a glass of wine. At the Ristorante Cappuccini Convento they serve them cooked with goats' cheese. This recipe originated from there.

SERVES 4

1kg (2lb) fresh broad beans	salt and pepper
2 large red onions	250g (8oz) soft, barely salted sheep
4 tablespoons olive oil	or goats' cheese

- Shell the broad beans.

- Roughly chop the onions. Heat the oil in a saucepan, add the onions and fry for 5-10 minutes until golden.

- Add the beans, stir for 1-2 minutes then cover with water and season with salt and pepper. Simmer for about 10 minutes until the beans are very tender and the liquid has evaporated.

- Cut the cheese into 8 thick slices and warm under the grill. Serve with the hot beans.

AUBERGINE ROLLS WITH MOZZARELLA

Yet another aubergine recipe, I hear you cry. Please try it, it is so good, particularly with the mozzarella cheese. Don't be tempted to pay extortionate prices for buffalo mozzarella cheese. The real thing should be eaten on the same day it is produced.

SERVES 6

1 very large aubergine weighing
    400-500g (14oz-1lb)
salt and pepper
4 tablespoons olive oil

250g (8oz) mozzarella cheese
8 fresh basil leaves
mixed green salad with black olives,
    to serve

- Thinly slice the aubergine, sprinkle the slices with salt, place in a bowl, cover and weigh down. Leave for 20 minutes. Rinse and pat dry.

- Heat the oil in a frying pan and fry the aubergine slices for about 3 minutes on each side until tender and slightly browned. Drain on kitchen paper.

- Slice the mozzarella cheese. Place a basil leaf on each slice then sprinkle with pepper. Roll each aubergine slice around a piece of cheese and place in a flameproof dish.

- Grill the aubergine rolls for about 4 minutes until the cheese softens. Serve immediately, with a salad.

PARMESAN POTATO PANCAKES

Whenever I think of potatoes I think of my Father, a real potato lover. Maybe it is to do with the fact that he grew Italian new potatoes and brought them into this country. I've grown up with him coming home and turning out of his pockets a handful of potatoes, which were quickly cooked for him to see if he approved of the flavour. If he did he was a happy man. This dish has many variations and can be served like a sandwich with, for example, creamy fresh spinach or cheese in the middle.

SERVES 4

2 large old potatoes	salt and pepper
75g (3oz) freshly grated Parmesan cheese	a little milk
	about 4 tablespoons olive oil
1 free range egg	fresh flat-leaved parsley, to garnish
25g (1oz) plain white flour	

- Peel then grate the potatoes into a bowl. Add the cheese, egg, flour, salt and pepper and enough milk to form a thick batter that is of a dropping consistency. Leave to stand for 15 minutes.

- In a large frying pan, heat the oil then drop in tablespoons of the mixture. Fry until golden brown on one side, turn and fry the second side until golden. Lower the heat and cook for a further 1-2 minutes. Drain on kitchen paper. Serve hot, garnished with parsley.

BAKED COURGETTES WITH PEPPERS

I first enjoyed this dish in Sicily, eating out of doors with the sun beating down, the smell of roasting peppers in the air and in the company of family and friends. What could be better in life?

SERVES 4

4 tender young courgettes	4 yellow or red peppers
salt and pepper	two 400g cans chopped tomatoes
2 garlic cloves	handful of torn fresh basil leaves
6 tablespoons olive oil	250g (8oz) mozzarella cheese

- Top and tail the courgettes then blanch in boiling salted water for 5 minutes. Drain and slice in half lengthways.

- Finely chop the garlic cloves. Heat 3 tablespoons of the oil in a frying pan, add the courgette slices and half the chopped garlic and fry for 8-10 minutes until golden.

- Grill the peppers under a hot grill until the skins are charred. Peel off the skins, cut the peppers in half, discard the core and seeds then slice the flesh.

- To make the tomato sauce, put the tomatoes with their juice, the remaining garlic and 2 tablespoons of the oil in a saucepan. Bring to the boil then simmer for 25 minutes. Add the basil, salt and pepper.

- Pre-heat the oven to 180°C, 350°F, Gas Mark 4. Grease an ovenproof dish.

- Slice the cheese. In the prepared dish, put a layer of half the courgettes, half the peppers, half the tomato sauce and half the cheese then repeat these layers. Sprinkle with the remaining oil.

- Bake in the oven for 20 minutes until the cheese has melted.

BULGARIAN POTATO PIE

This is another delicious potato recipe. To ring the changes, you could layer the potatoes with vegetables of your choice.

SERVES 4

2 medium onions	200ml (7fl oz) dry white wine
1kg (2lb) old potatoes	6 tablespoons breadcrumbs
about 8 tablespoons olive oil	salt and pepper
3 tablespoons tomato purée	

- Chop the onions. Peel and thinly slice the potatoes.

- Heat some of the oil in a deep frying pan, add some of the potatoes and fry gently for 10 minutes until browned. Using a slotted spoon, remove from the pan and cook the remaining potatoes, adding more oil if necessary. Remove from the pan.

- Add the onions to the pan and fry for 5 minutes until lightly brown. Add the tomato purée, the wine and 4 tablespoons breadcrumbs to make a thick but soft paste.

- Pre-heat the oven to 200°C, 400°F, Gas Mark 6. Brush an ovenproof dish with olive oil. Arrange a layer of potatoes in the prepared dish. Sprinkle with salt and pepper and spread over a layer of the onion and tomato mixture. Repeat these layers, seasoning the potatoes well each time. The final layer should be of onion and tomato.

- Sprinkle the top layer with 1 tablespoon of warm water, 1 tablespoon of olive oil and then a layer of the remaining breadcrumbs.

- Bake in the oven for 20 minutes until golden. Serve hot.

SWEET AND SOUR RED CABBAGE

There are many variations of this classic dish. Some recipes add caraway seed, some redcurrant jelly and it can be eaten hot or cold. It improves with re-heating and can be made a day in advance. This is my favourite version.

SERVES 4–6

1.5kg (3¼lb) red cabbage	75ml (3fl oz) white wine vinegar
65g (2½oz) butter	1 teaspoon salt
65g (2½oz) brown sugar	75ml (3fl oz) red wine

- Cut the cabbage into quarters. Remove the outer leaves and white core and wash well. Drain, dry and slice finely.

- Melt the butter in a large flameproof casserole. Add the cabbage and sugar and stir together. Add 75ml (3fl oz) water, the vinegar and salt. Cover and simmer for 30 minutes.

- Add the red wine. When the cabbage is tender, taste and adjust the seasoning if necessary. The flavour should be sweet and sour but not sharp. Serve hot.

ROSTI

This Swiss national dish is dedicated to a Swiss friend of mine, Kurt Haffner. There are however many variations. This is my favourite and I hope it will become yours too.

SERVES 4

800g (1¾lb) potatoes	125g (4oz) Emmenthal or Gruyère
salt and pepper	cheese
100g (4oz) unsalted butter	300ml (10fl oz) single cream

- Peel and grate the potatoes then sprinkle with salt.

- Melt the butter in a large heavy frying pan. Pile the potato into the pan and fry for 20 minutes, turning occasionally.

- Meanwhile, grate the cheese then stir in the cream. Halfway through cooking, add the cheese and cream. When the potatoes are tender, turn the Rösti on to a warmed serving plate and serve hot.

CEPES IN A CREAM SAUCE

This is a delicious simple vegetable dish, provided all the ingredients are at their very best. Do seek out the freshest of mushrooms. I smell them for a good earthy smell of the forest which indicates freshness.

SERVES 4

800g (1¾lb) fresh cèpes or flat mushrooms	1 garlic clove
salt and pepper	handful of flat-leaved parsley
1 medium onion	50g (2oz) butter
1 shallot	50ml (2fl oz) olive oil
	200ml (7fl oz) single cream

- Wipe the cèpes or mushrooms well and slice diagonally. Season with salt and pepper.

- Chop the onion, shallot, garlic and parsley.

- Heat the butter and oil in a frying pan until very hot. Fry the cèpes, a few at a time, until lightly browned. The fat must be very hot to let the cèpes fry quickly. Remove from the pan and drain on kitchen paper.

- Add the onion and shallot to the pan and fry for 3 minutes until lightly browned.

- Stir in the cooked cèpes, cream and garlic and simmer gently for 10 minutes. Sprinkle with the chopped parsley and serve immediately.

DAUPHINE POTATOES

Yet another potato dish but a stunning one at that. This is a classic dish from the Dauphiny region of France, which is well known for its gratin dishes. Be sure that the potatoes you use will remain firm during the cooking.

SERVES 4

900ml (1½ pints) milk	1 garlic clove
75g (3oz) butter	175ml (6fl oz) double cream
salt and pepper	freshly grated nutmeg
1kg (2lb) potatoes	50g (2oz) Gruyère cheese

- In a saucepan, boil the milk, add the butter and season with salt and pepper

- Peel the potatoes, wipe them but do not wash. Cut into slices 2-3 cm (¾-1¼ inch) thick. Crush the garlic.

- Put the slices in the boiling milk and add the garlic. Simmer for 20 minutes.

- Pre-heat the oven to 180°C, 350°F, Gas Mark 4. Butter an ovenproof dish.

- Add the cream to the potatoes and season with nutmeg. Transfer to the prepared dish. Grate the cheese and sprinkle on top.

- Cook in the oven for 15 minutes until well browned. Serve hot.

Fresh Salads

Light, refreshing, cleansing, appetizing – that is what a salad conjures up in my mind. There are so many interesting salad leaves to choose from today that there is no excuse for a boring, soggy salad any more. In Italy and other Mediterranean countries, salads are a cleansing course, always served as a course on its own. It is always my favourite part of a meal. I particularly enjoy simplicity, not forgetting the use of seasonings for the salad ingredients as well as the best quality extra virgin olive oil that you can afford. Serve the salads in this chapter on their own, as a main course, a starter or as an accompaniment to a main dish.

FRESH ORANGE, OLIVE AND SHERRY SALAD

There is a dazzling array of fruit grown in Spain and it is from there that this recipe originated! The market stalls all over the country display colourful arrangements of figs, melons, grapes, apples, dates, strawberries and, of course, oranges. This salad is light and fresh and if you use blood oranges they make it look very dramatic.

SERVES 4

4 large oranges
120ml (4fl oz) extra virgin olive oil
50ml (2fl oz) dry sherry
1 tablespoon chopped fresh mint

75g (3oz) black olives
salt and pepper
sprig of fresh mint, to garnish

- Using a sharp knife, peel the oranges, removing all the pith, so that the flesh of the oranges is revealed.

- Slice the oranges into rounds and arrange on a large flat serving plate.

- Drizzle over the oil and sherry then scatter with the mint and olives. Season with salt and pepper to taste and serve garnished with a sprig of mint.

LEMON, FENNEL AND ROCKET SALAD WITH RADICCHIO

I am particularly fond of this salad. Please don't be put off by the lemons, they really make it very delicious. Lemons grow profusely in the south of Italy and they're sweet enough to eat. Not only are they good for you, they're enormously versatile. I think a lemon will improve the flavour of any dish. I'm also a big fan of radicchio. My father is a major importer of radicchio which is grown in and around Verona.

SERVES 4

½ a radicchio (red chicory)
generous handful of rocket
2 large unwaxed lemons
1 fennel head
2 tablespoons extra virgin olive oil

2 tablespoons freshly grated
    Parmesan cheese
few drops of balsamic vinegar
salt and pepper

- Tear the radicchio into shreds. Tear the rocket. Peel and slice the lemons. Trim and slice the fennel into broad matchsticks.

- Arrange the radicchio on 4 individual plates. Add the lemon slices, fennel and torn rocket.

- To make the dressing, mix together the olive oil, Parmesan cheese, vinegar and salt and pepper to taste. Pour the dressing over the salad just before serving.

TOMATO AND MINT SALAD

*I remember this salad from a business trip in Sicily where family
friends served it for lunch. The flavours of the salad reflect the
Byzantine flavour of the region. The mint is so very typical and
blended with red onions makes a special flavour. Be discerning when
choosing tomatoes, I often find cherry tomatoes on the vine stalk have a
reliably good flavour as opposed to other varieties. Buy them firm and
with a bright colour. In Italy, Spain and France you can buy your
tomatoes in so many different degrees of ripeness. You will often be
asked if you want to eat them that day, the next day or use them to
make a sauce. I really enjoy being allowed to choose the different
tomatoes. To pick the best tomatoes, smell the stalk end – they should
smell peppery.*

SERVES 4

4 firm, bright red tomatoes
½ a small red onion
handful of fresh mint
salt and pepper
2 tablespoons fruity extra virgin

olive oil
25g (1oz) freshly grated Parmesan
   shavings
crusty or French bread, to serve

- Slice the tomatoes. Slice the onion into rings. Chop the mint.

- Arrange the tomatoes and onions on a serving plate then add the
mint.

- Season with salt and pepper to taste then pour over the olive oil.
Sprinkle over the Parmesan shavings and serve with bread.

FATTOUSH

There are so many variations of this Middle Eastern salad and I personally think this one is the best. It's a real meal salad – it's bright, crisp and crunchy all at once.

SERVES 4-6

For the salad
½ a cos lettuce
10 cherry tomatoes
5 stoned olives
5 spring onions
¼ of a cucumber
10 capers
1 tablespoon chopped fresh mint
1 tablespoon chopped fresh parsley

For the dressing
juice of ½ a lemon
2 tablespoons extra virgin olive oil
1 teaspoon herb or wholegrain
   mustard

For the croûtons
2 thin slices of bread
1 garlic clove
2 tablespoons olive oil
2 teaspoons chopped fresh mint

- Pre-heat the oven to 180°C, 350°F, Gas Mark 4.

- To prepare the salad, shred the lettuce, cut the tomatoes and olives in half, finely chop the spring onions and peel and dice the cucumber. Put all the salad ingredients in a large bowl and mix well together.

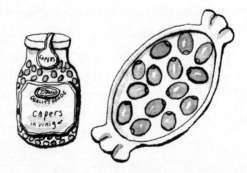

- To prepare the dressing, mix all the ingredients together.

- To prepare the croûtons, toast the bread slices. Crush the garlic and mix with the oil and mint. Brush the mixture over the slices of toast. Bake in the oven for 5 minutes. Cut off the crusts and cut the toast into small squares.

- Just before serving, mix the croûtons with the salad and pour over the dressing.

LEEKS WITH CORIANDER AND LEMON

This is a light and clean-tasting yet scented salad, rich with fruity oil. It makes an elegant salad for four as a starter or a lunch dish for two, served with lots of bread to soak up the fragrant juices. Oil, like lemon, is important to the character of the dish so do not stint on quality or quantity.

SERVES 4

8 long, thin young leeks
1 garlic clove
2 teaspoons coriander seeds
5 tablespoons extra virgin olive oil

pepper
grated rind and juice of 1½ lemons
handful of chopped fresh coriander
   leaves

- Trim and wash the leeks, leaving them whole. Choose a flameproof casserole or heavy-based saucepan that will hold the vegetables snugly in a single layer.

- Finely chop the garlic. Bruise the coriander seeds, put them into the casserole and toast over low heat. Add a generous 4 tablespoons of oil, the garlic and pepper. When the oil is warm, add the leeks. Turn them gently for 2-3 minutes.

- Mix the lemon rind and juice with 200ml (7fl oz) water and pour over the leeks. Bring to the boil, cover tightly and cook over a low heat for 20 minutes or until the leeks are tender. Turn them once or twice during the cooking.

- Transfer the leeks to a serving dish. Fast boil the cooking liquid for 2-3 minutes until reduced slightly and syrupy, adding a dash more oil if too tart.

- Pour the sauce over the leeks, leave until warm or cold, then scatter with the coriander leaves and serve.

CAPONATA

In Italy this is made in large quantities by most families and kept in clay pots, ready to be served as an accompaniment to cold meats and fish. I think that aubergines are a fantastic vegetable and in Italy are eaten in so many different ways. I have many recipes using them, which I hope you will enjoy throughout this book.

SERVES 4

4 medium aubergines	3 celery sticks
salt and pepper	1 tablespoon capers
4 tablespoons olive oil	50g (2oz) stoned green olives
1 onion	4 tablespoons wine vinegar
400g can chopped tomatoes, drained	1 tablespoon sugar

- Cut the aubergine into cubes. Sprinkle with salt, place in a bowl, cover and weigh down. Leave for 20 minutes.

- Rinse the aubergine cubes and pat dry. Heat 3 tablespoons of the oil in a frying pan and fry the cubes for about 5 minutes until brown and tender. Drain on kitchen paper.

- Slice the onion. Heat the remaining 1 tablespoon of oil in a saucepan, add the onion and fry for 5 minutes until golden. Add the tomatoes, salt and pepper and simmer for 15 minutes.

- Slice the celery into 2.5cm (1 inch) pieces. Rinse the capers and olives under cold water. Add to the tomato sauce with the vinegar and sugar. Simmer for a further 15 minutes until reduced slightly, stirring occasionally.

- Put the aubergine in a serving dish and stir in the sauce. Leave for at least 30 minutes before serving.

MY PANZANELLA

There are so many variations of this original Tuscan salad. It is ideal for a summer party or to have in your fridge to eat when hunger strikes. Every time I make this, it is always well received.

SERVES 4-6

2 red peppers
2 yellow peppers
6 plum tomatoes
handful of flat-leaved fresh parsley
handful of fresh basil leaves
10 stoned black olives

2 tablespoons capers
½ a ciabatta loaf
8 tablespoons fruity extra virgin
  olive oil
2 tablespoons red wine vinegar
salt and pepper

- Pre-heat the oven to 200°C, 400°F, Gas Mark 6.

- Put the peppers on a baking tray and roast for 20 minutes until blistered and deflated. Leave to cool.

- Meanwhile, put the tomatoes in a bowl, cover with boiling water for about 30 seconds then plunge into cold water. Using a sharp knife, peel off the skins then roughly chop the flesh, discarding the seeds.

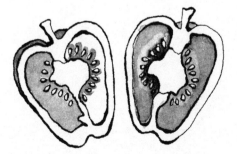

- Chop the parsley. Tear the basil leaves. Cut the olives in half. Rinse and chop the capers.

- Cut the bread into 1cm (½ inch) cubes and put in a bowl then drizzle over half the oil.

- Cut the cooled peppers in half and roughly chop the flesh, discarding the core and seeds.

- Add the peppers to the bread with the tomatoes, parsley, basil, olives, capers, vinegar and remaining oil. Season well with salt and pepper and mix well together before serving.

FRENCH COUNTRY SALAD

This hearty salad is full of goodness and the beans and potatoes together make it substantial.

SERVES 6

450g (1lb) French beans
450g (1lb) new potatoes
salt and pepper
1 small red onion
50g (2oz) French stoned black olives

handful of flat-leaved fresh parsley
400g can haricot beans, drained
1 tablespoon capers
4 tablespoons extra virgin olive oil
2 tablespoons lemon juice

- Steam the French beans for 15 minutes until tender. Cook the potatoes in boiling salted water for 10-15 minutes until tender.

- Meanwhile, finely chop the onion. Slice the olives. Finely chop the parsley.

- Cut the cooked beans into 2.5cm (1 inch) lengths. Drain the potatoes and cut into small cubes.

- In a salad bowl, mix together the potatoes, French beans, haricot beans, onion, olives and capers.

- Whisk together the oil, lemon juice, salt and pepper. Pour the dressing over the salad and toss well together.

- Sprinkle with the parsley and serve at room temperature.

BURGHUL AND TOMATO SALAD

Also known as Tabouleh, this salad has become very popular in this country. It is traditionally Lebanese and is a mountain dish that has become a national dish. Burghul wheat is a terrific store cupboard standby, as not only does it cook quickly but adds great texture to casseroles. I often just pour boiling water over the wheat, leave it to swell and cook and just add extra virgin olive oil, chopped spinach, tomato and garlic.

SERVES 4

125g (4oz) burghul wheat
1 onion
6 tomatoes
250g (8oz) flat-leaved fresh parsley
handful of fresh mint
2 garlic cloves

juice of 1½-2 lemons (according to your taste)
6 tablespoons extra virgin olive oil
cos lettuce leaves, to serve
salt and pepper

- Put the burghul wheat in a large bowl, cover with boiling water and place a clean tea-towel over the top. Leave to soak for 15 minutes.

- Meanwhile, finely chop the onion, chop the tomatoes, finely chop the parsley and mint and crush the garlic.

- Line a sieve with muslin or a clean tea-towel. Pour the burghul wheat into the sieve and allow to drain then squeeze the cloth to extract as much liquid as possible from the wheat.

- Tip the burghul wheat into a bowl and add all the remaining ingredients. Mix together and leave for 10 minutes to allow the flavours to blend.

- Serve with crisp cos leaves to scoop up the salad.

SPINACH AND YOGURT SALAD

These two flavours go remarkably well together. Use young, tender spinach leaves as these can be eaten raw, as in this salad, and you do not have to remove the stalks

SERVES 4

1kg (2lb) fresh, tender, young spinach
1 garlic clove

150 ml (¼ pint) natural yogurt
salt and pepper

- Wash the spinach and put in a large salad bowl.

- Crush the garlic and add to the yogurt with salt and pepper. Pour over the spinach and serve.

SALAD OF ROASTED PEPPERS

This salad is eaten all over Europe. In my Grandmother's kitchen it was always available as it can be stored in jars and preserved as a salad for your store cupboard.

SERVES 4

2 yellow peppers
2 red peppers
3 tablespoons extra virgin olive oil
1 tablespoon balsamic vinegar

salt and pepper
1 garlic clove (optional)
a few sprigs of fresh oregano, to garnish

- Pre-heat the oven to 200°C, 400°F, Gas Mark 6.

- Put the peppers in a roasting tin and bake in the oven for 25 minutes until blistered and slightly charred. Leave to cool.

- When cool, hold the peppers over a bowl, to reserve the juice, and peel off the skins. Cut the flesh into thin strips and put in a serving dish.

- Add the oil, vinegar, salt and pepper to the pepper juice and whisk together. If using, crush the garlic and add to the dressing.

- Pour the dressing over the peppers and serve garnished with sprigs of oregano.

MRS F'S SALAD

Made by my Mother in a hurry one day, this is established as a firm family favourite.

SERVES 4

2 celery sticks
2 carrots
6 cherry tomatoes
1 small red onion
handful of flat-leaved fresh parsley

handful of fresh mint
3 tablespoons extra virgin olive oil
1 tablespoon lemon juice
salt and pepper

- Roughly chop the celery. Peel and roughly chop the carrots. Cut the tomatoes in half. Chop the onion. Chop the parsley and mint.

- Put all the ingredients in a bowl. Mix together and serve the salad immediately.

CRUNCHY GORGONZOLA CROSTINI SALAD

I am very keen on Gorgonzola cheese – and blue cheese is very good for you because the natural penicillin present in it boosts your immune system and keeps you strong. So don't jump to your medicine chest if you are feeling run down. I love lemons too, hence the dressing. I think they are also good for you so I should really call this recipe Medicinal Salad.

SERVES 4

4 slices of ciabatta bread
2 tablespoons olive oil
1 cos lettuce
3 tablespoons strong, peppery, extra virgin olive oil
grated rind and juice of 1 unwaxed

lemon
salt and pepper
1 garlic clove
100g (4oz) Gorgonzola cheese
1 tablespoon stoned black olives

- Pre-heat the oven to 200°C, 400°F, Gas Mark 6.

- Brush the bread slices with olive oil and bake in the oven for 10 minutes until golden but not too crunchy.

- Wash the lettuce, dry well and tear the leaves into shreds. Put in a salad bowl.

- To prepare the dressing, whisk together the extra virgin olive oil, lemon rind and juice, salt and pepper.

- Cut the garlic clove in half. Cut the cheese into cubes.

- Assemble the crostini by rubbing the garlic over the bread and spreading the cheese on the bread. Cut the crostini into bite-sized pieces.

- Toss the crostini into the lettuce. Add the olives and pour over the dressing. Toss the salad together until well mixed then serve immediately.

BEETROOT SALAD

When discussing the writing of this book with my Mother, she politely requested a beetroot salad as it is one of her favourite vegetables. My work has taken me to Sweden, from where this recipe originated, as beetroot is enormously popular in Scandinavian countries.

SERVES 4-6

450g (1lb) even-size beetroot
salt and pepper
1 garlic clove
2 tablespoons red wine vinegar
4 tablespoons light and fruity extra

virgin olive oil
1 small onion
handful of flat-leaved fresh parsley
handful of torn basil leaves

- Wash the beetroots well and cook in boiling salted water for about 20 minutes until tender.

- Slip the skins off the beetroots and chop into rough cubes.

- Crush the garlic. Add the vinegar, oil, salt and pepper and whisk together. Pour over the beetroot while still warm so that the dressing will be well absorbed.

- Slice the onion into rings and use to garnish the beetroot with the parsley and basil, before serving.

GREEN BEAN SALAD

This salad has to be the simplest salad of all. Please use home grown or organic beans as they will always have the very best flavour.

SERVES 4

450g (1lb) green beans
salt and pepper
2 tablespoons extra virgin olive oil

grated rind of 1 unwaxed lemon
and 1 tablespoon lemon juice

- Wash the beans then top and tail them. Cook in boiling salted water for 8-10 minutes until tender. Drain and leave to cool.

- Whisk together the oil, lemon rind and juice, salt and pepper. Pour over the beans and serve warm.

'ONLY GOODNESS' COLESLAW SALAD

This is a salad from my first business, 'Only Goodness'. Cabbage is as excellent raw as it is cooked and combines well with other ingredients. I suggest experimenting with flavours such as grated coconut, chopped almonds, peanuts or beans.

SERVES 4

100g (4oz) sunflower seeds
350g (12oz) white cabbage
2 carrots
100g (4oz) Gruyère cheese

2 eating apples
juice of 1 lemon
3 tablespoons extra virgin olive oil
salt and pepper

- Spread the sunflower seeds on a sheet of foil and grill until golden, stirring frequently.

- Finely shred the cabbage. Grate the carrots. Dice the cheese. Core and cut the apple flesh into cubes.

- In a serving bowl, put the cabbage, carrot, cheese, apple and sunflower seeds and mix well together.

- Whisk together the lemon juice, oil, salt and pepper. Pour the dressing over and toss together. Serve immediately.

Main Courses

I have designed this chapter with dishes that can be proudly served and enjoyed as a course in their own right. Nevertheless, they still are not time-consuming and can be made in and around 30 minutes. Many illustrate the importance of vegetables and I have included pasta and rice dishes, too. These recipes are some of my most trusted and popular with family and friends. They are nutritious, rich and tasty and yet not difficult.

PASTA SHELLS WITH WILD MUSHROOM SAUCE

This recipe comes from the Parma region of Italy. It is wonderfully light, luscious and super-quick.

SERVES 4-6

50g (2oz) dried wild mushrooms (preferably porcini)
450g (1lb) pasta shells
75g (3oz) walnuts
handful of fresh basil leaves
handful of fresh sage leaves
200ml (7fl oz) single cream
salt and pepper
1 garlic clove
25g (1oz) unsalted butter
50g (2oz) freshly grated Parmesan cheese

- Soak the mushrooms in water for 10 minutes.

- Meanwhile, cook the pasta in a large saucepan of boiling water for 10-12 minutes until just tender.

- Finely chop the walnuts, basil and sage. Add to the cream with salt and pepper and mix together.

- Crush the garlic. Drain the mushrooms and pat dry. Melt the butter in a frying pan. Add the garlic and fry gently for 2-3 minutes.

- Drain the cooked pasta and add the mushrooms. Now quickly add the cream sauce, stirring all the time. Serve sprinkled with the Parmesan cheese.

AUBERGINE CANNELLONI

This recipe illustrates yet again the versatility of aubergines. It is really popular with my nieces and nephews who are all very young.

SERVES 2

2 aubergines, each weighing about 250g (9oz)
salt and pepper
75ml (3fl oz) olive oil
225g (8oz) ricotta
50g (2oz) freshly grated Parmesan cheese, plus extra to garnish
handful of finely torn fresh basil leaves
1 quantity of Tomato Sauce, to serve (see page 205)

- Thinly slice the aubergines lengthways, discarding the ends and rounded pieces from the sides. Sprinkle the slices with salt, place in a bowl, cover and weigh down. Leave for 15 minutes. Rinse the slices and pat dry.

- Heat 2-3 tablespoons of oil in a large, non-stick frying pan. Add a single layer of aubergine slices and fry over medium heat for about 5 minutes until light golden on both sides. Remove from the pan and drain on kitchen paper. Repeat with more oil and the remaining aubergine slices.

- Put the ricotta, Parmesan cheese, basil and salt and pepper to taste in a bowl and beat well together.

- Put the aubergine slices on a work surface. Spoon the cheese mixture along the length of the aubergines then roll up the slices to form about 12 cannelloni.

- Serve with the tomato sauce and sprinkle with Parmesan cheese.

ROASTED FENNEL AND TOMATO SAUCE WITH CONCHIGLIE

The fennel and tomato complement each other so well in this recipe. I hope it will become a firm favourite.

SERVES 6

1 medium fennel head
3 tablespoons olive oil
1 garlic clove
400g can chopped tomatoes
grated rind of 1 unwaxed lemon

salt and pepper
450g (1lb) conchiglie (pasta shells)
freshly grated Parmesan cheese, to
  serve

- Pre-heat the oven to 200°C, 400°F, Gas Mark 6.

- Remove the fennel's tough outer leaves, trim and wash well. Cut into lengths and steam or cook in boiling water for 7-8 minutes until tender. Transfer to a roasting tin and drizzle over 1 tablespoon of oil. Roast in the oven for 20 minutes until golden.

- Meanwhile, crush the garlic. Heat the remaining 2 tablespoons of oil in a saucepan, add the garlic and fry gently. Add the tomatoes and lemon rind and cook gently for 25 minutes.

- Chop the cooked fennel into small pieces and add to the sauce. Season with salt and pepper and heat gently.

- Cook the pasta in a large saucepan of boiling water for about 10 minutes until just tender.

- When the pasta is cooked, drain and toss with the sauce. Serve hot with freshly grated Parmesan cheese.

MALFATTI

The title of this recipe translates as 'badly made' and implies that the dumplings don't all have to be made the perfect shape and size. Enjoy this dish when fresh spinach is in season as frozen spinach is too wet to use. It is guaranteed to please everyone that eats it. Serve Malfatti with vegetables in season or a salad.

SERVES 6

2kg (4lb) spinach leaves
500g (1lb) ricotta
2 large free range eggs
125g (4oz) freshly grated Parmesan cheese

salt and pepper
pinch of freshly grated nutmeg
flour, for coating
75g (3oz) butter

- Wash the spinach leaves and remove the stems. Put in a large saucepan with only the water still clinging to the leaves after washing. Cover and cook for 5 minutes until they crumple, turning once or twice. Drain through a sieve and squeeze every bit of water out with your hands. (This is very important and is the secret of success, otherwise they fall apart.) Finely chop the leaves.

- Mash the ricotta in a bowl then stir in the eggs, half the Parmesan cheese, salt, pepper, nutmeg and spinach. Mix together very well, then shape into balls the size of a walnut and roll in the flour.

- Half-fill a large pan with water, bring to the boil and carefully drop in the dumplings. Keep the water barely simmering until they rise to the surface. Using a slotted spoon, very carefully lift out the dumplings and place on warmed plates.

- Melt the butter and pour over the dumplings. Sprinkle with the remaining cheese and serve hot.

BAKED PASTA AND SPINACH PIE

In Italy this pie is cut into little pieces and eaten on feast days and at celebrations. It is sold throughout Italy in many shapes and forms. It is my favourite recipe and has been handed down to me by my Grandmother. It can be kept for two days in the fridge, is excellent either hot or cold and is a good idea for picnics.

SERVES 4

For the pasta
450g (1lb) strong white flour
   (preferably 'OO' grade pasta
   flour)
1 teaspoon salt
3 free range eggs
1 teaspoon olive oil
4 teaspoons warmed milk
beaten egg, to glaze

For the spinach filling
1kg (2lb) fresh spinach
salt and pepper
½ tsp freshly grated nutmeg
3 free range eggs
100g (4oz) ricotta
50g (2oz) freshly grated Parmesan
   cheese
1 teaspoon olive oil

- To make the pasta, put the flour and salt on a work surface and make a well in the centre.

- Beat the eggs and oil together then put in the well. Carefully and gradually draw in the flour from the inside of the well and gradually add the milk until the mixture resembles a coarse dough. Knead for about 10 minutes to form a smooth, firm, soft dough. Wrap and leave to rest in the fridge for 10 minutes.

- Meanwhile, make the filling. Wash the spinach leaves and remove the stems. Put in a large saucepan with only the water still clinging to the leaves after washing. Cover and cook for 5 minutes until they crumple. Drain the spinach through a sieve, squeezing out as much liquid as possible.

- Put in a bowl, add all the remaining ingredients and mix together.

- On a floured surface, knead the dough again for 5-10 minutes until it is smooth and elastic. Leave it, covered, for a further 5 minutes.

- Pre-heat the oven to 200°C, 400°F, Gas Mark 6. Lightly oil 2 baking trays.

- Divide the dough into 4 pieces and roll them out thinly. Line each tray with a piece of dough, letting the sides overhang. Spread generously with the spinach filling.

- Use the remaining pieces of dough to cover the filling. Make a small slit in the middle of the top. Take the two layers of pasta hanging over the sides and gently press them together round the edge.

- Brush with beaten egg and bake in the oven for about 20 minutes until golden brown.

COUSCOUS WITH SEVEN VEGETABLE SAUCE

Couscous is the national dish of Morocco. In Morocco it is more delicate and less hot and spicy than the Tunisian and Algerian versions now found in France. Seven, considered a lucky number, is the traditional number of vegetables used in the recipe, the choice depending on those in season. This is a one-pot meal, easy to make for large numbers. It does actually take longer than 30 minutes to prepare but I simply had to include it.

SERVES 5-6

For the Seven Vegetable Sauce
125g (4oz) chick-peas, soaked
    overnight
2 large onions
2 garlic cloves
½ teaspoon saffron
2 teaspoons cinnamon
1 teaspoon paprika
a large pinch of cayenne
½ teaspoon ground ginger
salt
large bunch of fresh parsley,
    chopped
large bunch of fresh coriander,
    chopped
1 tablespoon olive oil
125g (4oz) raisins
Choose 7 vegetables from the

following:-
225g (8oz) carrots, cut in half
    lengthways
½ medium white cabbage, cut into
    8 pieces
6 artichoke hearts
1 medium aubergine, quartered
225g (8oz) small potatoes
225g (8oz) turnips, sliced
225g (8oz) broad beans, shelled
225g (8oz) piece of pumpkin, cut
    into 5cm (2 inch) slices
2 tomatoes
For the couscous
450g (1lb) pre-cooked couscous
pinch of salt
2 tablespoons olive oil
15-25g (½-1oz) butter

- To prepare the sauce, drain the chick-peas and put in a large saucepan. Add 3 litres (5 pints) of water, bring to the boil and remove the froth. Finely chop the onions and garlic and add to the pan with the spices. Simmer for at least 30 minutes.

- Add the salt when the chick-peas begin to soften.

- Add the carrots, cabbage, artichoke hearts, aubergines and potatoes and more water if necessary and cook for 20 minutes. Add the turnips, broad beans and raisins and cook for 10 minutes. Add the pumpkin and tomatoes and cook for 5 minutes. Add the herbs and oil cook for further 5 minutes.

- Whilst the vegetables are cooking, prepare the couscous. Put the couscous in a large bowl and pour in 300ml (½ pint) of water with the salt. Stir well until evenly absorbed. Leave for 10 minutes.

- Add a further 300ml (½ pint) of water and the oil and butter. Rub the grain between your palms and make sure that all the grains are separate. Leave for a further 10 minutes until the grains are swollen and tender but separate.

- Steam the couscous, uncovered, in the top half of a steamer over boiling water for about 8 minutes. (When the steam begins to come through the grain it is ready to serve.)

- Turn the cooked couscous on to a large warmed serving dish and crush with a fork to separate the grains. Put the vegetables in the centre and serve immediately.

ITALIAN ROASTED RED PEPPER PLAIT

This makes an impressive dish, full of good flavours and colours. I've demonstrated it so many times because it not only looks good but is simple, wholesome and tasty. It is even good reheated the next day.

SERVES 6

1 red pepper
75g (3oz) pine kernels
500g (1lb) fresh spinach
1 medium onion
1 garlic clove
250g (8oz) mushrooms
handful of flat-leaved parsley
3 fresh plum tomatoes

1 teaspoon olive oil
pinch of freshly grated nutmeg
pepper
250g (8oz) puff pastry
125g (4oz) dolcelatte or
   Gorgonzola cheese (optional)
beaten egg, to glaze
sesame seeds, to garnish

- Pre-heat the oven to 200°C, 400°F, Gas Mark 6. Grease a
  30 × 20cm (12 × 8 inch) baking tray.

- Roast the pepper in the oven for 20 minutes until the skin blisters,
  turning occasionally. Peel off the skin and chop the flesh into 1 cm
  (½ inch) pieces, discarding the core and seeds.

- Toast the pine kernels in the oven for 5 minutes until golden.

- Wash the spinach and remove the stems. Put in a large saucepan
  with only the water still clinging to the leaves after washing. Cover
  and cook for 5 minutes. Drain well, keeping the leaves as whole as
  possible.

- Finely chop the onion. Crush the garlic. Slice the mushrooms.
  Chop the parsley. Put the tomatoes in a bowl, cover with boiling
  water for about 30 seconds then plunge into cold water. Using a
  sharp knife, peel off the skins then chop the flesh.

- In a large frying pan, heat the oil. Add the onion, garlic and mushrooms. Remove from the heat and add the chopped pepper, pine kernels, spinach, parsley and tomatoes. Season with the nutmeg and pepper.

- On a lightly floured surface, roll out the pastry to a 28 x 18cm (11 x 7 inch) rectangle and place on the baking tray. Place the filling down the centre and top with sliced dolcelatte or Gorgonzola cheese, if using.

- Cut the pastry on either side of the filling into 2.5cm (1 inch) diagonal strips, leaving at least 1 cm (½ inch) uncut on either side of the filling. Use the strips to overlap the filling to form a plait.

- Brush with the beaten egg and sprinkle with sesame seeds. Bake in the oven for about 20 minutes until golden.

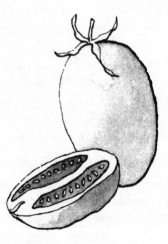

ALMOND AND MUSHROOM-STUFFED CABBAGE LEAVES WITH CREAMY CIDER SAUCE

This is a deliciously satisfying dish. I like the contrast of the rich green leaves with the sauce. Do use good mushrooms, preferably organic for maximum flavour. I always buy my mushrooms from a stall on the Portobello Road. Brian, the stall owner, always says when he sees me 'mushrooms, I've got some extra good ones today!'.

SERVES 4

1 small savoy cabbage
1 garlic clove
225g (8oz) leeks
100g (4oz) flat or brown cap mushrooms
25g (1oz) butter
100g (4oz) chopped almonds
2-3 teaspoons lemon juice
2 teaspoons paprika
2 teaspoons dill weed

1 free range egg
salt and pepper
150ml (¼ pint) vegetable stock (see page 209)
For the sauce
1 medium onion
15g (½oz) butter
300ml (½ pint) dry cider
75ml (3fl oz) single cream
1 teaspoon lemon juice

- Select 8 good coloured leaves from the cabbage and blanch or steam them for 4-5 minutes to soften. Remove the central stalk if very tough.

- Finely chop 225g (8oz) of the remaining cabbage. Finely chop the garlic, leeks and mushrooms

- Melt the butter in a large frying pan. Add the garlic, leeks, mushrooms and chopped cabbage and fry gently for 10 minutes.

- Pre-heat the oven to 200°C, 400°F, Gas Mark 6.

- Add the chopped almonds, lemon juice, paprika and dill weed to the leek mixture and cook over a low heat for 5 minutes. Allow to cool slightly. Beat the egg and add with salt and pepper.

- Divide the stuffing between the leaves and roll up tightly, tucking in the sides as you roll. Pack the rolled leaves into an ovenproof dish, add the stock and cover with foil.

- Bake in the oven for 20 minutes.

- Meanwhile, make the sauce. Finely chop the onion. Melt the butter in a saucepan. Add the onion and fry for 5-10 minutes until golden brown. Add the cider and bring to a simmer then cook for 2-3 minutes.

- Allow to cool slightly then blend in a food processor or blender until smooth.

- Pour the cream into a clean pan and gradually stir in the blended sauce. Add the lemon juice, salt and pepper and stir well together.

- Reheat the sauce gently but do NOT boil, stirring all the time.

- Serve the cabbage leaves with the hot creamy cider sauce.

PANZAROTTI

These fried pastries are very adaptable so do feel free to use different fillings, for example fresh spinach and ricotta. If, in the unlikely event, they are not eaten the day they are made, they can be reheated in a warm oven.

SERVES 4-6

For the dough
450g (1lb) plain white flour
4 free range eggs
4 tablespoons olive oil
salt
olive oil, for frying
For the filling
225g (8oz) ricotta

2 large free range eggs
100g (4oz) dolcelatte cheese
handful of chopped fresh parsley
225g (8oz) mozzarella cheese
100g (4oz) freshly grated Parmesan
   cheese
salt and pepper

- To make the dough, put the flour in a bowl, make a well in the centre and break in the eggs. Add the oil and salt. Using a fork, draw in the flour from the inside of the well, gradually adding more flour until the mixture resembles a coarse dough. Knead for about 10 minutes to form a smooth, elastic dough. Wrap and leave to rest in the fridge for 10 minutes.

- Meanwhile, make the filling by mixing together all the filling ingredients.

- On a lightly floured surface, roll the dough as thinly as you can. Using a teaplate, cut into rounds. Place spoonfuls of the filling on the rounds 1cm (½ inch) from the edge. Fold into half-moon shapes and seal the edges together decoratively. Leave to rest in the fridge for 10 minutes.

- Heat the oil in a frying pan to a depth of 1cm (½ inch). When hot, lower a few at a time into the oil and cook for 2-3 minutes until golden. Using a slotted spoon, remove from the pan and drain. Serve immediately.

RISOTTO WITH ASPARAGUS, FENNEL, LEMON AND MINT

Please do use asparagus in season where possible. It cannot be bettered for flavour. Do use fennel that is long and thin as it is less stringy. This rather encapsulates all my favourite flavours. I cannot emphasise enough the usefulness of risotto. It is a one-pan meal that is made in 20-30 minutes. It's nutritious and tasty and makes use of your store cupboard and leftovers in the fridge. You can really put your hallmark of individualism into a risotto. A risotto does not reheat, it must be made and eaten at that moment, just like pasta.

SERVES 4

700g (1½lb) young fresh asparagus
6 medium shallots
350g (12oz) fennel
100g (4oz) unsalted butter
2 tablespoons olive oil
1 litre (1¾ pints) vegetable stock
   (see page 209)
350g (12oz) arborio (risotto) rice

grated rind and juice of 1 unwaxed
   lemon
handful of chopped fresh mint plus
   sprigs, to garnish
1 wine glass of dry white wine
150g (5oz) freshly grated Parmesan
   cheese plus shavings, to serve
salt and pepper

- Trim the asparagus stalks then simmer in boiling water for 3 minutes. Drain, refresh in cold water, drain again and set aside.

- Chop the shallots. Finely slice the fennel. Melt the butter and oil in a medium saucepan, add the shallots and fry for 5 minutes until softened. Add the fennel and fry for a further 2-3 minutes.

- Meanwhile, bring the stock to the boil and keep just below simmering point.

- Add the rice to the pan and stir well together.

- Add the stock, a ladleful at a time, until it has been absorbed. Stir well between each addition, adding the lemon rind and juice at this stage, until the rice is tender but still firm. This will take 20-30 minutes depending on the quality of the rice.

- Meanwhile, slice the asparagus. About 10 minutes towards the end of the cooking add the asparagus, mint, wine and grated cheese.

- Season with salt and pepper. (If you add salt at the beginning of making the risotto it makes the rice tough and it will not absorb any liquid.) Serve immediately, garnished with Parmesan cheese shavings and mint leaves.

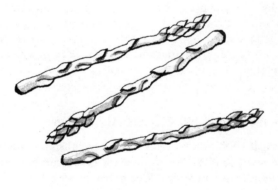

GRUYERE AND THYME SOUFFLE

*After consulting my friend about the suitability of a soufflé in my book,
I was greeted with a resounding yes. Each friend has their own story of
how they like their soufflé. I was surprised at their reaction because I
was sure they would say 'oh no, definitely 1960's food'. Although I
know I love soufflés, I thought I was in the minority. A soufflé is
definitely right for my book. It's certainly quick, it's spectacular and
it's tasty. Gruyère and thyme is just one idea for this soufflé. Feel free to
experiment with other ingredients. Any blue cheese is good and
mushrooms, rosemary and puréed asparagus are also good.*

SERVES 4

40g (1½oz) butter
breadcrumbs, for dusting
100g (4oz) Gruyère cheese
25g (1oz) plain flour
1 teaspoon wholegrain mustard
pinch of cayenne

pinch of paprika
1 tablespoon fresh thyme
salt and pepper
300ml (½ pint) full cream milk
4 free range eggs, separated

- Pre-heat the oven to 200°C, 400°F, Gas Mark 6.

- Melt a small knob of the butter and use to brush the inside of a
  15cm (6 inch) soufflé dish. Sprinkle the breadcrumbs over to cover
  the sides and base of the dish. Grate the cheese.

- Melt the remaining butter in a saucepan, stir in the flour, mustard,
  cayenne, paprika, thyme and pepper. Cook for at least 30 seconds,
  stirring all the time with a wooden spoon, until the mixture
  becomes pale and steams.

- Add the milk gradually (if you have warmed the milk it is better)
  and cook, stirring continuously, for 3 minutes until the mixture is
  thick.

- Stir in the cheese, egg yolks, salt and more pepper to taste.

- Whisk the egg whites until stiff, but not dry. Using a metal spoon, fold the egg whites into the mixture, spoonful by spoonful.

- Pour into the prepared soufflé dish. Run your finger around the top of the soufflé mixture. This gives a 'top hat' effect to the cooked soufflé.

- Bake in the oven for 25 minutes. If the soufflé wobbles still, cook for a further 5 minutes. Serve immediately.

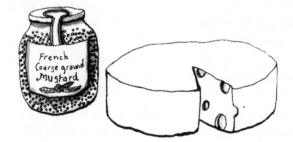

PASTA WITH AUBERGINES, WINE AND CREAMY TOMATO SAUCE

This recipe just happened one day. Looking in the fridge, suddenly a new recipe evolved. Do experiment, you might like to add courgettes or red peppers.

SERVES 4

1 medium ripe aubergine
salt and pepper
3 tablespoons olive oil
4 tablespoons red wine
1 small onion
½ a garlic clove
½ carton of creamed tomatoes
(passata) or a 400g can chopped tomatoes
275g (10oz) penne or any other shaped pasta
2 tablespoons double cream
3 tablespoons finely chopped fresh oregano

- Cut the aubergine into cubes. Sprinkle with salt, place in a bowl, cover and weigh down. Leave for 15 minutes.

- Rinse the aubergine cubes well and pat dry. Heat the oil in a frying pan, add the aubergine and fry for 5 minutes until golden. Add the wine and simmer for 15 minutes.

- Meanwhile, finely chop the onion and crush the garlic. Add the onion, garlic and tomatoes to the aubergine, bring up to the boil then simmer for 10 minutes.

- Cook the pasta in boiling salted water for 10 minutes until just tender.

- Just before serving, stir the cream and oregano into the sauce. Drain the pasta and toss with the sauce. Serve hot.

COURGETTE AND BARLEY GRATIN

This has proved a very popular recipe. As a consultant, I worked with Habitat and this particular recipe was popular. I think that barley is a really underrated grain. It accepts flavours well and is a definite plus for the store cupboard. This dish looks attractive if you arrange the courgettes overlapping each other on the top of the dish.

SERVES 4

225g (8oz) pearl barley
1 litre (1¾ pint) vegetable stock
  (see page 209)
450g (1lb) courgettes
2 garlic cloves
3 tablespoons olive oil
50g (2oz) unsalted butter
6 ripe tomatoes

150g (5oz) mozzarella cheese
handful of torn basil leaves
handful of chopped fresh mint
150g (5oz) freshly grated Parmesan
  cheese
salt and pepper
50g (2oz) fresh white breadcrumbs

- In a large saucepan, cook the barley in the vegetable stock for about 20 minutes, until most of the stock has been absorbed.

- Meanwhile, thinly slice the courgettes. Crush the garlic. Heat the oil and butter in a frying pan, add the courgettes and garlic and fry for 5 minutes until golden. Drain and reserve.

- Chop the tomatoes and mozzarella cheese and add to the barley, with the basil, mint and Parmesan cheese. Season well with salt and pepper to taste.

- Pre-heat the oven to 200°C, 400°F, Gas Mark 6.

- To assemble, arrange half the courgettes in a shallow ovenproof dish in a neat layer. Now add the barley mixture, then a neat layer of courgettes. Sprinkle over the breadcrumbs.

- Bake in the oven for 15 minutes until golden. Serve hot.

WILD MUSHROOM AND BASIL TART

I first enjoyed this tart in Florence many years ago. It is full of flavour and is ideal picnic food when you've worked up a good appetite out of doors. It's also relatively quick to make after work.

SERVES 6

50g (2oz) dried porcini
250g (8oz) fresh mushrooms
1 medium onion
50g (2oz) butter
salt and pepper
3 free range eggs
150ml (5fl oz) soured cream or

mascarpone cheese
50g (2oz) freshly grated Parmesan cheese
3 tablespoons fresh torn basil leaves
250g (8oz) shortcrust pastry (see page 212)

- Soak the dried mushrooms in boiling water for 10 minutes. Squeeze dry then chop finely. Chop the fresh mushrooms and the onion.

- Melt the butter in a frying pan, add the onion and salt and fry for 5 minutes until golden. Add the dried and fresh mushrooms and continue cooking for 5 minutes. Remove from the heat and add pepper.

- In a large bowl, put the eggs, soured cream or mascarpone cheese, the Parmesan cheese, basil, salt and pepper, and whisk together. Add the cooked mushroom and onion mixture.

- Pre-heat the oven to 200°C, 400°F, Gas Mark 6.

- On a lightly floured surface roll out the pastry and use to line a 20cm (8 inch) metal flan ring or tin. Line with foil or greaseproof paper and weigh down with baking beans. Bake blind in the oven for 10-15 minutes until the sides of the pastry are crisp. Remove the lining and beans.

- Pour in the egg and mushroom mixture and bake for 20 minutes until set.

CHIVE AND POPPY SEED CREPES

This recipe was requested by my Mother who works miracles with crêpes and her Grandchildren just love them. They fit in well with busy lives as they are so versatile. You can roll them up with so many fillings such as spinach, onion and ricotta, cheese sauce with thyme, tomato sauce with basil and all types of vegetables. Just experiment, anyway.

MAKES 8

175g (6oz) plain white flour
salt and pepper
2 teaspoons poppy seeds
handful of snipped fresh chives
2 large free range eggs

450ml (¾ pint) full cream milk
25g (1oz) unsalted butter
cheese or tomato sauce, to serve
   (see pages 204 and 205)

- In a large bowl, mix the flour, a pinch of salt, pepper, poppy seeds and chives. Make a well in the centre and break in the eggs. Add half the milk and gradually draw in the flour from the inside of the well.

- Melt the butter. Add half the melted butter to the remaining milk, then add to the flour mixture and mix well together.

- Over a medium heat, melt a little of the remaining butter in a heavy based 18cm (7 inch) crêpe or frying pan. When hot but not burning, pour in just enough batter to cover the bottom of the pan thinly. Cook for 1-2 minutes until the mixture bubbles and the base is golden. Flip over and cook until the second side is golden.

- Serve as soon as they are cooked with the sauce on top.

CREAMY CHILLI AND TOMATO BAKE WITH HERBS

*Make this recipe when tomatoes are at their best. It is simple and very,
very tasty. Serve with rich red wine and crusty bread.*

SERVES 4-6

2 onions
1 small red chilli
1 large garlic clove
700g (1½lb) fresh ripe tomatoes
4 tablespoons olive oil
handful of torn fresh sage and basil
   leaves, plus leaves to garnish

salt and pepper
6 free range eggs
50g (2oz) ricotta
125g (4oz) freshly grated
   marzolina, Parmesan or pecorino
   cheese

- Pre-heat the oven to 200°C, 400°F, Gas Mark 6.

- Finely chop the onions and chilli, discarding the seeds as they are
  the hottest part. Crush the garlic. Roughly chop the tomatoes,
  discarding the seeds.

- Heat the oil in a medium saucepan, add the onions, chilli and garlic
  and cook for 5 minutes until the onion softens and browns. Add
  the tomatoes and cook for 3 minutes. Add the herbs, salt and
  pepper.

- Mix together the eggs, ricotta and half of the cheese. Put the
  tomato mixture in a shallow ovenproof dish and pour over the egg
  mixture. Sprinkle over the remaining cheese.

- Bake in the oven for 20 minutes until golden brown. Serve
  garnished with chopped herbs.

PROVENÇAL VEGETABLES WITH GOATS' CHEESE DRESSING

This dish captures the flavours of Provence. Do be sure to use good goats' cheese. I tend to use a mild cheese so as not to interfere with the flavours of the vegetables. I like to serve the vegetables just warm so that the flavour of the dressing is absorbed.

SERVES 4

6 ripe tomatoes
75g (3oz) mild goats' cheese
1 garlic clove
4 tablespoons olive oil
1 tablespoon lemon juice
salt and pepper

handful of pine kernels, to garnish
100g (4oz) broccoli florets
100g (4oz) French beans
100g (4oz) mange-tout
2 small courgettes

- To make the dressing, put the tomatoes in a bowl, cover with boiling water for about 30 seconds then plunge into cold water. Using a sharp knife, peel off the skins then roughly chop the flesh, discarding the seeds.

- Put the tomatoes, goats' cheese, garlic, olive oil, lemon juice, salt and pepper in a food processor and blend the ingredients together until smooth.

- Spread the pine kernels on a sheet of foil and toast under the grill, turning them frequently. Set aside.

- In a large saucepan of boiling salted water, blanch the vegetables in batches until just tender but still very firm to the bite. Allow about 6-7 minutes for the broccoli, 5 minutes for the beans and 2 minutes for the mange-tout and courgettes. Remove from the pan with a slotted spoon and drain each batch of vegetables well.

- To serve, pour the dressing over the vegetables and garnish with the pine kernels.

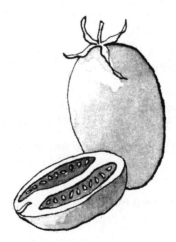

POTATO GNOCCHI

I just had to include this recipe. It's not only a classical recipe but, done well, totally memorable. This is for my Father, who loves potatoes. I recommend you make this dish with a helper in the kitchen, it's more fun and the job is done with ease.

SERVES 4

900g (2lb) even sized old potatoes
1 free range egg
salt
50g (2oz) butter
225-275g (8-10oz) plain flour

Tomato Sauce, to serve (see page 205)
freshly grated Parmesan cheese, to serve

- Cook the potatoes, in their skins, in boiling water for 20 minutes until tender. Drain well and when cool enough to handle, peel off the skins.

- Push the potatoes through a sieve, on to a work surface, from a height to enable the potato to fall and lighten with air.

- Beat the egg and add to the potato with plenty of salt, the butter and half the flour. Mix well with a light touch. Knead until soft, adding more flour if necessary.

- With floured hands, roll the dough into 2.5cm (1 inch) thick rolls then cut into pieces about 2cm (¾ inch) long.

- Press a finger into each piece to flatten then draw your finger towards you to curl the sides.

- Bring a large pan of salted water to the boil and drop in about 20 gnocchi. Lower the heat and cook gently for 2-3 minutes, allowing the gnocchi to pop to the top of the pan and counting for 30 seconds. Remove with a slotted spoon and keep warm. Repeat with the remaining gnocchi.

- When all the gnocchi are cooked, toss in the tomato sauce and serve sprinkled with Parmesan cheese.

SOUTHERN ITALIAN LAYERED POTATO PIE

This dish is a distant relation to Paella and comes from Apulia in southern Italy. In Apulia the land is rich and produces delicious potatoes. This recipe is a typical dish of the region. I have a great many family friends living there and love their food.

SERVES 4

900g (2lb) new potatoes
salt and pepper
4 onions
2 garlic cloves
225g (8oz) flat mushrooms
2 tablespoons olive oil

225g (8oz) mozzarella cheese
25g (1oz) breadcrumbs
2 tablespoons chopped fresh parsley
handful of torn fresh basil leaves
100g (4oz) freshly grated Parmesan
   cheese

- Scrub and slice the potatoes into 5mm (¼ inch) thick slices. Cook in a large pan of boiling salted water for 10-15 minutes until tender. Drain.

- Pre-heat the oven to 200°C, 400°F, Gas Mark 6.

- Finely chop the onions. Crush the garlic. Slice the mushrooms. Heat the oil in a frying pan, add the onions and fry for 5-10 minutes until golden. Add the garlic and cook for a further 1 minute. Add the mushrooms and cook for a further 2 minutes. Season with salt and pepper.

- Slice the mozzarella cheese. In a shallow ovenproof dish, sprinkle over half the breadcrumbs. Add a layer of mushrooms, sprinkle over half the parsley and basil and add a layer of mozzarella cheese, Parmesan cheese and potatoes. Repeat these layers, finishing with a layer of potatoes. Sprinkle over the remaining breadcrumbs.

- Bake in the oven for 20 minutes until golden and bubbling. Serve straight from the oven.

PASTA WITH SEVEN WILD HERBS

I recently invented this dish whilst teaching in Italy. I wandered into the garden and stumbled across some wild herbs and so the recipe came about.

SERVES 4

500g (1lb) spaghetti or tagliatelle
125g (4oz) mixture of fresh mint, parsley, marjoram, basil, sage, oregano and rosemary, plus extra to garnish
5 ripe tomatoes

3 tablespoons extra virgin olive oil
2 tablespoons ricotta
2 tablespoons freshly grated Parmesan cheese
salt and pepper

- Cook the pasta in the usual way (see glossary).

- Meanwhile, very finely chop the herbs. Finely chop the tomatoes, discarding the seeds. Put the herbs, tomatoes, oil, ricotta, Parmesan cheese, salt and pepper in a bowl and mix together to form a paste.

- Drain the cooked pasta, add the herb sauce and toss together. Serve garnished with the extra herbs.

ROCKET AND CHEESE POLENTA

Polenta is a real favourite of mine as readers of my last book, Pizza, Pasta and Polenta, *will know. It does take a little time to prepare but the result is worthwhile. Please don't be tempted to use pre-cooked or ready made polenta as both are poor substitutes.*

SERVES 4

1 litre (1¾ pints) vegetable stock (see page 209) or water
salt and pepper
200g (7oz) coarse polenta
generous handful of chopped fresh
rocket
75g (3oz) freshly grated Parmesan cheese
50g (2oz) butter

- In a large saucepan, bring the stock or water and 1 teaspoon salt to the boil. Gradually add the polenta, letting it run through your fingers in a thin stream, stirring constantly to prevent lumps forming.

- Simmer the polenta for 30-40 minutes until the mixture comes away from the sides of the pan, stirring frequently.

- When the polenta is cooked, stir in the rocket, Parmesan cheese, butter and pepper. Serve hot.

ASPARAGUS AND BASIL PANCAKES

Following my mother's request for pancakes and Susanna's (my editor) request for a recipe using the surplus asparagus in her garden, this recipe is for them.

SERVES 4

For the pancakes
125g (4oz) plain white flour
pinch of salt
1 free range egg
300ml (½ pint) milk
olive oil, for frying
For the filling
500g (1lb) asparagus

2 shallots
2 tablespoons olive oil
½ quantity of Béchamel Sauce (see page 203)
generous handful of fresh basil
freshly grated Parmesan cheese, to serve (optional)

- To make the pancake batter, put the flour and salt in a bowl and make a well in the centre. Beat the egg and add to the flour with the milk then beat together to form a smooth batter.

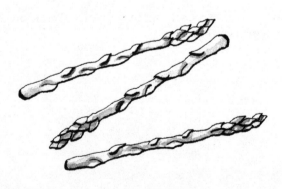

- Pre-heat the oven to 200°C, 400°F, Gas Mark 6.

- Trim the asparagus and put on a baking tray. Finely chop the shallots and sprinkle on top of the asparagus then drizzle over the oil. Roast in the oven for 10-15 minutes until tender.

- Meanwhile, make the Béchamel Sauce as described in the recipe. Finely tear the basil leaves, add to the sauce and keep warm.

- To cook the pancakes, heat a spoonful of oil in a medium frying pan and when hot, add a ladleful of the batter. Fry on both sides until golden brown. Drain on kitchen paper. Repeat, heating the pan each time, to make 8 pancakes. Stack the pancakes between sheets of greaseproof paper and keep warm.

- To serve, add a dollop of sauce to each pancake, put some of the asparagus and shallots in the middle and roll up. Sprinkle Parmesan cheese on top, if wished.

SPAGHETTI WITH BLACK OLIVES

When I was writing my second book I conducted a survey in Italy. I found that spaghetti was the favourite shaped pasta and this particular sauce was the most popular.

SERVES 4

1 garlic clove
1 red pepper
100g (4oz) stoned black olives
7 tablespoons olive oil

400g can chopped tomatoes
1 tablespoon capers (optional)
salt and pepper
500g (1lb) spaghetti

- Thinly slice the garlic. Cut the pepper into quarters then chop the flesh, discarding the core and seeds. Cut the olives in half.

- Heat the oil in a medium saucepan, add the garlic and pepper and cook gently for 5 minutes until softened but not browned.

- Add the tomatoes, olives, capers, if using, and pepper. Cover and simmer for 10 minutes.

- Meanwhile, cook the spaghetti in a large pan of boiling salted water until just tender.

- Drain the cooked spaghetti, add the hot sauce and toss together. Serve immediately.

Cooking for Friends

The recipes in this chapter are rather more special than those in other chapters but definitely not complicated. They are dishes for informal entertaining and many can be made for parties and celebrations, too. All are easy to make so that you don't have to spend hours in the kitchen but you will have time to be with your friends.

FETTUCINE WITH CREAM AND PEAS

The green and yellow colours of the pasta with the peas and cheese, make this an elegant dish for a dinner party. In fact I think fettucine is the most suitable pasta to serve with a creamy sauce for a special occasion.

SERVES 4

4 shallots
50g (2oz) butter
1 tablespoon olive oil
175ml (6fl oz) single cream
225g (8oz) shelled fresh peas

50g (2oz) freshly grated Parmesan cheese
salt and pepper
225g (8oz) yellow fettucine
225g (8oz) green fettucine

- Finely chop the shallots. Melt the butter with the oil in a medium-sized saucepan, add the shallots and fry for 5 minutes until lightly golden.

- Add the cream and cook gently over a low heat until the cream starts to thicken. Add the peas and half the Parmesan cheese. Cook on a low heat for 10 minutes.

- Bring a large pan of water to the boil, add salt and the yellow pasta then the green. (The green pasta will cook more quickly.) Cook until just tender.

- Drain the pasta and put in a warmed dish. Season with salt and pepper, add the sauce and mix well together. Add the remaining Parmesan cheese and serve immediately.

RICOTTA AND GORGONZOLA GNOCCHI

This is a dish to impress and is light, despite the rich ingredients. It was given to me by the owners of a restaurant in Volpago del Montello.

SERVES 6

400g (14oz) ricotta
2 tablespoons freshly grated
    Parmesan cheese
3 egg yolks
2 tablespoons semolina
large pinch of freshly grated
    nutmeg

salt and pepper
15g (½oz) butter
2 tablespoons double cream
100g (4oz) Gorgonzola cheese
1 tablespoon chopped fresh flat-
    leaved parsley

• Mash the ricotta with the Parmesan cheese, egg yolks, semolina, nutmeg, salt and pepper and mix well together.

- On a lightly oiled surface, roll the paste into thin rolls about 1cm (½ inch) in diameter, then cut with a sharp knife into pieces about 2 cm (¾ inch) long.

- Melt the butter with the cream in a saucepan. Add the Gorgonzola cheese and cook over a very low heat, crushing and stirring the cheese until you have a smooth sauce.

- Bring a large pan of water to the boil then drop in the gnocchi and simmer for about 2 minutes or until they rise to the surface. Using a slotted spoon, lift them out and transfer to a warmed dish.

- Serve hot, with the sauce poured over and sprinkled with parsley.

RIGATONI WITH CHEESE SAUCE

Rigatoni is the best pasta to use in this recipe as its ridges help the sauce to cling to it. I find it a particular favourite with children as they love the pasta tubes.

SERVES 4

450g (1lb) rigatoni
300ml (½ pint) Béchamel sauce
  (see page 203)

50g (2oz) freshly grated Parmesan
  cheese
2 tablespoons breadcrumbs

- Cook the pasta in a large saucepan of boiling water for about 10 minutes until tender.

- Meanwhile, prepare the béchamel sauce. Stir in 25g (1oz) of the cheese.

- Drain the pasta and put into a shallow ovenproof dish. Pour the sauce over the pasta. Mix together the remaining cheese and breadcrumbs and sprinkle on top.

- Put under a hot grill until the top is golden brown and crispy. Serve hot.

PISSALADIERE

This famous onion tart of Nice derives its name from the anchovy paste, pissala, which used to be brushed on it. Now the traditional anchovy garnish is more often absent while the thick onion filling has become even thicker. I like to use the smaller quantity of onion given in the recipe but the Niçois prefer the larger amount. It is ideal for an alfresco lunch with friends and a good bottle of wine.

SERVES 6

½ quantity of shortcrust pastry (see page 212)
1-2kg (2-4lb) onions
3-4 tablespoons olive oil
salt and pepper

2 teaspoons chopped fresh mixed herbs, such as thyme and rosemary
a few stoned black olives

- Pre-heat the oven to 200°C, 400°F, Gas Mark 6.

- On a lightly floured surface, roll out the pastry and use to line a 20cm (8 inch) plain flan ring or tin. Line with foil or greaseproof paper and weigh down with baking beans. Bake blind in the oven for 15 minutes until the sides of the pastry are crisp. Remove the lining and beans and return to the oven for 5 minutes to crisp the bottom.

- Meanwhile, make the filling. Slice the onions. Heat the oil in a saucepan, add the onions, cover and cook over a low heat, stirring occasionally, for 20 minutes or until they are very soft. Add the salt, pepper and herbs and continue to cook for 2-3 minutes. Put the filling in the pastry case.

- Bake in the oven for 20 minutes until golden. Halve the olives and use to garnish the tart.

CELEBRATION PIZZAS

These pizzas remind me of Minori, my Grandparent's home. They are always eaten on special occasions and can be bought in pastry shops throughout Italy.

MAKES 6

500g (1lb) fresh or frozen puff pastry, or 1 quantity of Rough Puff Pastry (see page 213)
1 quantity of Tomato Sauce (see page 205)

handful of torn fresh basil leaves
two 225g (8oz) packets mozzarella cheese
salt and pepper

- Pre-heat the oven to 220°C, 425°F, Gas Mark 7.

- On a lightly floured surface, roll out the pastry and, using a saucer or small plate, cut into six 10-12.5cm (4-5 inch) circles.

- Spread with a small amount of the tomato sauce and put some torn basil on each. Grate the cheese and sprinkle on top. Season with salt and pepper.

- Bake in the oven for 10 minutes until golden.

TOMATO TART

This is so simple and yet so impressive. It can be made in moments but gives the appearance of a great deal of effort. Please do buy the best, firm red tomatoes that you can find – even better if they are home grown.

SERVES 4-6

750g (1½lb) firm ripe tomatoes
250g (8oz) frozen puff pastry,
   thawed
125g (4oz) Gruyère cheese
25g (1oz) butter

4 tablespoons double cream
2 free range eggs
salt and pepper
handful of torn fresh basil leaves

- Put the tomatoes in a bowl, cover with boiling water for about 30 seconds then plunge into cold water. Peel off the skins then cut into quarters. Hold the quarters over a colander and squeeze gently to remove excess liquid. Chop the flesh and leave to drain in the colander for 10 minutes.

- Pre-heat the oven to 220°C, 425°F, Gas Mark 7. Pre-heat a heavy baking tray.

- On a lightly floured surface, thinly roll out the pastry and use to line a 23-25cm (9-10 inch) fluted tart tin fitted with a removable base. Grate the cheese and sprinkle 25g (1oz) of cheese over the pastry base.

- Put the butter in a bowl and beat until soft then work the remaining cheese and cream into the butter to form a fluffy paste. Beat the eggs then beat into the mixture. Season lightly with salt and pepper and add the basil.

- Season the tomatoes with salt and pepper and spread evenly over the pastry case. Spoon the egg and cheese mixture over the tomatoes.

- Place the tart on the baking tray and cook in the oven for 15 minutes. Reduce the oven temperature to 180°C, 350°F, Gas Mark 4 and bake for 10-15 minutes until the filling is puffed and richly coloured and the pastry is crisp. Serve hot, cold or warm.

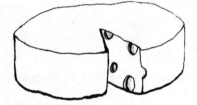

MARINATED GOATS' CHEESE

These days you see large jars of tiny cheese in olive oil on the counters of many delicatessens. It is more fun to prepare them yourself and to create your own personal combination of herbs. They make excellent presents for friends at birthdays, Christmas or just a 'thank you' gift.

MAKES 1 JAR

small round goats' cheese each weighing about 50g (2oz)
a selection of flavourings such as rosemary sprigs, garlic cloves, bay leaves, thyme sprigs, small shallots, black olives, chilli peppers and peppercorns
olive oil

- Loosely pack the goats' cheese into a jar. Tuck in your choice of flavourings and cover with oil.

- Cover and store in a cool dry place for at least 2 weeks before using.

HERB, WALNUT AND CHEESE LOAF

This sounds a typical '60s vegetarian dish but it's not. It is ideal for an impromptu party for friends, alfresco lunch and picnics.

SERVES 4-6

250g (8oz) tomatoes	1 tablespoon chopped fresh thyme
125g (4oz) mature Cheddar cheese	salt and pepper
1 onion	1 egg
250g (8oz) ground walnuts	

- Pre-heat the oven to 200°C, 400°F, Gas Mark 6. Grease a 500g (1lb) loaf tin.

- Put the tomatoes in a bowl, cover with boiling water for about 30 seconds then plunge into cold water. Peel off the skins then slice thinly. Grate the cheese. Finely chop the onion.

- Put the tomatoes, cheese, onion, walnuts, thyme, salt and pepper in a bowl. Beat the egg, add to the mixture and mix together. Spoon the mixture into the prepared tin and press down well.

- Bake in the oven for 20 minutes until set. Leave to cool before turning out and serving.

FENNEL, TOMATO AND SPINACH PANCAKES

This is a great dish to prepare ahead of time for your friends.

SERVES 4

For the filling
500g (1lb) fresh spinach
6 tomatoes
1 fennel head
½ an onion
25g (1oz) butter
handful of chopped fresh basil
salt and pepper

25g (1oz) fresh white breadcrumbs
For the pancakes
125g (4oz) plain flour
¼ teaspoon salt
1 egg
300ml (½ pint) milk
olive oil, for frying

* To make the filling, wash the spinach and put in a saucepan with only the water still clinging to the leaves after washing. Cook for 5 minutes then drain well, squeezing out the excess water. Finely chop the spinach.

- Put the tomatoes in a bowl, cover with boiling water and leave for 30 seconds then plunge into cold water. Peel off the skins then roughly chop the flesh, discarding the seeds.

- Trim and finely chop the fennel and onion. Heat the butter in a medium saucepan and add the fennel, onion, basil, salt and pepper. Cook for 5 minutes then add the spinach, tomatoes and breadcrumbs.

- To make the pancakes, sift the flour and salt into a bowl. Make a well in the centre, beat the egg and add with half of the milk. Gradually mix the flour into the liquid to make a smooth batter. Stir in the remaining milk.

- Grease a 20cm (8 inch) frying pan with a little oil then pour in enough batter to cover the bottom of the pan, tilting the pan so that the batter covers it evenly. Cook over a moderate heat until the bottom of the pancake is golden brown. Flip the pancake over and cook the other side briefly. Keep the pancake warm while making 7 more pancakes in the same way.

- Pre-heat the oven to 200°C, 400°F, Gas Mark 6. Grease an ovenproof dish. Divide the filling between the pancakes. Roll up the pancakes and arrange side by side in the prepared dish.

- Cover with foil and cook in the oven for 10 minutes until hot.

MOUSSAKA WITH RICE

This was immensely popular in my first restaurant, 'As You Like It'. It is a warming dish, ideal for a cold winter day.

SERVES 4-6

250g (8oz) long grain white rice
1 medium aubergine
salt and pepper
2 large potatoes
4 garlic cloves
1 onion
400g can tomatoes

6 tablespoons olive oil
25g (1oz) butter, preferably
    unsalted
2 tablespoons plain white flour
250ml (8fl oz) milk
pinch of freshly grated nutmeg
6 allspice berries

- Wash the rice and leave to soak in fresh water. Slice the aubergine. Sprinkle with salt, place in a bowl, cover and weigh down. Peel and thinly slice the potatoes. Finely chop the garlic and onion.

- Drain the rice and put in a saucepan with the tomatoes, garlic, onion and ½ teaspoon of salt and pepper to taste. Add 225ml (8fl oz) of water and simmer gently for 15-20 minutes until the liquid is absorbed.

- Rinse and dry the aubergine slices. Heat 3 tablespoons of oil in a frying pan, add the aubergine and fry for 5 minutes until golden. Drain and set aside.

- Rinse and dry the potato slices. Heat the remaining oil in a frying pan, add the potatoes and fry for 10 minutes until golden. Drain and set aside.

- To make the white sauce, gently heat the butter in a small saucepan, stir in the flour and cook gently, stirring, for 1 minute. Remove from the heat and gradually stir in the milk until smooth. Slowly bring to the boil, stirring constantly, until the sauce boils and thickens. Add the grated nutmeg, salt and pepper and simmer for 1 minute.

- Pre-heat the oven to 190°C, 375°F, Gas Mark 5. Grease a shallow ovenproof dish.

- In the prepared dish, put in a layer of potatoes, then aubergines then a layer of rice. Space out the allspice berries on top of the rice. Pour over the sauce.

- Bake in the oven for about 20 minutes until golden. Serve hot.

RICOTTA AND HERB STUFFED COURGETTES

This dish looks really impressive with the courgettes filled widthways as opposed to lengthways and yet couldn't be easier. Serve with a crisp salad or as a vegetable course on its own. I often teach this dish and it is always well received.

SERVES 6

6 medium courgettes
50g (2oz) mozzarella cheese
25g (1oz) day old breadcrumbs
125g (4oz) ricotta
3 tablespoons freshly grated
   Parmesan cheese

handful of torn fresh basil leaves
2 teaspoons fresh thyme
salt and pepper
1 egg white
olive oil, for brushing

- Pre-heat the oven to 200°C, 400°F, Gas Mark 6.

- Bring a medium saucepan of water to the boil. Add the courgettes and boil for 5 minutes then plunge them into cold water and pat dry.

- Cut almost through each courgette widthways, at 2cm (¼ inch) intervals, taking care not to cut right through.

- Meanwhile, make the filling. Finely chop the mozzarella cheese and mix with the breadcrumbs, ricotta, Parmesan cheese, basil, thyme, salt and pepper. Lightly beat the egg white, stir into the mixture and mix well together.

- Place some filling in each courgette and put in a shallow ovenproof baking dish.

- Lightly brush with oil and cook in the oven for 15 minutes until golden brown. Serve hot.

LAYERED MOZZARELLA AND TOMATO BAKE

This is a colourful and tasty dish. The tomatoes do take time to prepare but it is all worthwhile.

SERVES 4

1 small onion
1 garlic clove
1 tablespoon olive oil
400g can chopped tomatoes
salt and pepper
750 (1½lb) young courgettes

2 tablespoons plain flour
25g (1oz) butter
250g (8oz) mozzarella cheese
handful of torn fresh basil
50g (2oz) freshly grated Parmesan
   cheese

- Pre-heat the oven to 200°C, 400°F, Gas Mark 6.

- Chop the onion. Crush the garlic. Heat the olive oil in a small saucepan. Add the onion and garlic and fry for 5 minutes.

- Stir in the tomatoes, salt and pepper and bring to the boil. Lower the heat, half cover with a lid and simmer for 10-15 minutes until the sauce has thickened.

- Cut the courgettes into matchsticks, 2.5cm (1 inch) long. Coat in the flour. Heat the butter in a frying pan, add the courgettes and fry for 2-3 minutes until browned.

- Coarsely grate the mozzarella cheese. In a shallow ovenproof dish, put the courgettes, then half the mozzarella, then the tomato mixture with a handful of basil sprinkled on top. Finally, add a layer of the remaining mozzarella. Sprinkle the Parmesan cheese over the top.

- Bake in the oven for 10-12 minutes until hot.

TAGLIATELLE WITH GORGONZOLA SAUCE

This is a real favourite for me – it's a very classical sauce found on most menus up and down the length of Italy. This is a dish with which to impress your friends.

SERVES 4

350g (12oz) tagliatelle
25g (1oz) unsalted butter
175g (6oz) Gorgonzola cheese
150ml (¼ pint) whipping cream

2 tablespoons dry white wine
1 tablespoon chopped fresh sage
salt and pepper

- Cook the pasta in a large saucepan of boiling water until just tender.

- Meanwhile, make the sauce. Melt the butter in a medium saucepan. Crumble in the Gorgonzola cheese and gently stir until melted. Pour in the cream and wine and mix vigorously. Add the sage, salt and pepper and stir until the sauce thickens. Set aside.

- Drain the cooked pasta and stir in the sauce. Toss well together and serve immediately.

COURGETTE, MINT AND TOMATO GOUGERE

Light and delicious, do make this dish when courgettes are plentiful and in season. It looks very impressive at a dinner party.

SERVES 4

2 onions
1 red pepper
350g (12oz) young courgettes
250g (8oz) tomatoes
2 tablespoons olive oil
handful of chopped fresh mint
salt and pepper

25g (1oz) freshly grated Parmesan cheese
For the choux pastry
65g (2½oz) plain flour
pinch of salt
50g (2oz) butter
2 free range eggs

- Chop the onions. Slice the pepper, discarding the core and seeds. Slice the courgettes. Cut the tomatoes into quarters, discarding the seeds.

- Heat the oil in a large frying pan, add the onion, pepper, courgettes, tomatoes, mint, salt and pepper and cook for 10 minutes.

- Pre-heat the oven to 200°C, 400°F, Gas Mark 6.

- To make the choux pastry, sift the flour and salt together on to a sheet of greaseproof paper.

- Melt the butter in a saucepan, add the 150ml (¼ pint) water and bring to the boil. When bubbling, remove the pan from the heat and immediately add the flour, all at once. Beat the mixture until it is smooth and leaves the sides of the pan clean. Allow to cool slightly.

- Beat the eggs and gradually add to the mixture, beating well between each addition.

- Spoon the choux pastry around the edge of a shallow 1.4 litre (2½ pint) ovenproof dish. Turn the vegetable mixture into the centre and sprinkle with the Parmesan cheese.

- Cook in the oven for 20 minutes until golden brown and risen. Serve immediately.

PASTA WITH HERBED RICOTTA SAUCE

This is light and refreshing and goes well with tagliatelle. It's made in moments and so is ideal for unexpected guests. Do feel free to change the herbs.

SERVES 4

350g (12oz) pasta, such as tagliatelle
1 egg yolk
150g (5oz) ricotta
90ml (3fl oz) double cream

4 tablespoons freshly grated Parmesan cheese
handful of chopped fresh parsley
salt and pepper
handful of torn fresh basil

- Cook the pasta in a large saucepan of boiling water until just tender.

- Meanwhile, beat together the egg yolk and ricotta until smooth.

- Heat the cream in a saucepan, stir in the Parmesan cheese and parsley and season with salt and pepper to taste. Beat in the ricotta mixture.

- Drain the cooked pasta, stir in the sauce and basil leaves and toss well together. Serve immediately.

FALAFEL

Falafel are spiced chick-pea balls, Middle Eastern in origin. Serve with a generous wedge of lemon, green salad and warmed pitta bread. They are very portable and ideal for so many occasions. I have memories of making literally thousands, with help of course, at an open day at the Cordon Vert Cookery School. I can remember that there was no surface in the kitchen without falafels but within an hour they had all been demolished.

SERVES 4-6

450g (1lb) chick-peas, soaked overnight
3 garlic cloves
2 teaspoons coriander
2 teaspoons cumin
2 tablespoons chopped fresh parsley

salt and pepper
olive oil, for frying
lemon wedges, to garnish
Minted Yogurt Sauce, to serve (see page 206)

- Drain the chick-peas from the soaking water. Put in a saucepan, cover with fresh water and bring to the boil. Boil rapidly for 10 minutes, reduce the heat then simmer for 20 minutes until tender. (If the chick-peas are old they will take longer.) Drain the chick-peas.

- In a food processor, finely chop the garlic. Add the chick-peas, coriander, cumin, parsley, salt and pepper and blend until smooth. Remove from the bowl and form into a ball the size of a large chestnut then flatten slightly.

- Heat the oil in a frying pan and fry the falafels in batches for 2-3 minutes until golden brown all over. Drain well and serve hot with lemon wedges and Minted Yogurt Sauce.

BEAN HOT POT

This dish is ideal for the winter months and is even better eaten the following day as the flavours develop.

SERVES 6

1 onion	two 400g cans cannellini beans,
4 potatoes	drained
2 garlic cloves	400g can tomatoes
3 tablespoons olive oil	salt and pepper
1 tablespoon finely chopped fresh	freshly grated Parmesan cheese, to
sage	serve
2 red peppers	crusty bread, to serve
2 courgettes	

- Finely chop the onion. Peel and cut the potatoes into small cubes. Crush the garlic.

- Heat the oil in a saucepan, add the onion and cook for 5 minutes until softened. Add the potatoes, garlic and sage and cook until the potatoes soften. (This will depend on the size of the potatoes.)

- Meanwhile, finely slice the peppers, discarding the core and seeds. Cut the courgettes into matchsticks.

- When the potatoes are soft, stir in the peppers, courgettes, beans and tomatoes. Bring to the boil then simmer, uncovered, for 15 minutes.

- Season well with salt and pepper and serve with Parmesan cheese and crusty bread.

SPINACH, GREEN PEA AND RICOTTA GNOCCHI

I have so many recipes for gnocchi, each one as good as the next. I love the colour and texture of this particular recipe. Do be sure to use fresh peas as their flavour is infinitely superior. I first enjoyed this gnocchi in Verona a year ago, eating with some family friends.

SERVES 4

225g (8oz) fresh spinach leaves
225g (8oz) shelled fresh peas
1 tablespoon torn fresh sage plus
   leaves to garnish
2 free range eggs
200g (7oz) ricotta

pinch of freshly grated nutmeg
salt and pepper
75g (3oz) freshly grated Parmesan
   cheese
3 tablespoons breadcrumbs
5 tablespoons plain flour

- Wash the spinach leaves and remove the stems. Put in a large saucepan with only the water still clinging to the leaves after washing. Cover and cook for 2 minutes until wilted. Drain through a sieve and squeeze until dry.

- Cook the peas in a little water for about 8 minutes until just tender. Drain well.

- Put the spinach, sage and peas in a food processor and chop finely.

- Lightly beat the eggs and add to the spinach mixture with the ricotta, nutmeg, salt, pepper, half the Parmesan cheese, breadcrumbs and nearly all the flour. Mix well together, adding more flour if necessary. (The mixture should be firm enough for a spoon to stand upright in it.)

- Using well-floured hands take a heaped dessertspoonful of mixture and roll lightly into small ovals.

- Bring a large saucepan of water to the boil, then reduce the heat. Drop a few gnocchi at a time into the water and cook for 4-5 minutes or until they rise to the surface. Using a slotted spoon, remove from the pan and drain. Put in a warmed serving dish, cover and keep warm.

- Melt the butter with the sage leaves and pour over the gnocchi. Serve sprinkled with the remaining Parmesan cheese.

RISOTTO WITH PORCINI

This risotto can be made almost entirely from ingredients in the store cupboard. However, there are a few golden rules. Please use good stock, home-made of course and the correct rice – arborio.

SERVES 4

50g (2oz) dried porcini	350g (12oz) arborio (risotto) rice
6 medium shallots	1 wine glass of dry white wine
handful of fresh parsley	handful of torn fresh basil leaves
1.1 litres (2 pints) vegetable stock	50g (2oz) freshly grated Parmesan
(see page 209)	cheese
25g (1oz) unsalted butter	salt and pepper
2 tablespoons olive oil	

- Soak the mushrooms in 300ml (½ pint) hot water for 10 minutes.

- Meanwhile, finely chop the shallots and parsley. Bring the stock to the boil and keep just below simmering point.

- Heat the butter and oil in a medium saucepan, add the shallots and fry for 5 minutes until lightly coloured. Add the rice and cook for 2 minutes.

- Drain the mushrooms, retaining the water. Add a ladleful of stock to the rice and when it has almost been absorbed, add the mushrooms. Now add just under a ladleful of the reserved water from the mushrooms and the wine and cook until they have been absorbed. Continue adding the stock, stirring between each addition, until the rice is tender but firm. This will take about 20 minutes.

- Stir in the parsley, basil and Parmesan cheese. Season with salt and pepper to taste and serve immediately.

RISOTTO ALLA MILANESE

This is the classic risotto of Lombardy and is served as any part of a meal with a meat or vegetable course to follow. I often talk to my sisters and ask what they are cooking for their families dinner. Risotto is always on the agenda. Children love it as well as adults.

SERVES 4

6 shallots	(see page 209)
150g (5oz) unsalted butter	350g (12oz) arborio (risotto) rice
2 tablespoons olive oil	¼ teaspoon saffron powder
salt and pepper	100g (4oz) freshly grated Parmesan
7 tablespoons dry white wine	cheese
1 litre (1¾ pints) vegetable stock	4 tablespoons single cream

- Finely chop the shallots. Melt the butter and oil in a medium saucepan. Add the shallots and pepper and fry for 5 minutes until softened. Add the wine and 7 tablespoons of stock. Boil until reduced by half.

- Meanwhile, bring the stock to the boil and keep just below simmering point.

- Add the rice and cook for 5 minutes, stirring constantly. Add the saffron and the hot stock, a ladleful at a time, stirring well between each addition, until the rice is tender but firm. This will take about 20 minutes.

- Remove from the heat, add salt to taste, the cheese and cream. Leave to stand for 1 minute before serving.

Sweet Treats

Some of my all-time favourites are included in this chapter. There are
ice creams, puddings, pastries, cakes and preserves. Many of these
recipes take longer than 30-40 minutes to prepare but they can be
made in advance and left to cook whilst you are preparing the rest of
the meal. Ice creams, in particular, obviously take time to freeze but
they can be prepared in stages and you don't have to watch them. An
ice cream maker will, of course, speed up the process. All the recipes
are worth the extra effort.

CATALAN CREAM

This light, aromatic cream is popular in the region of Catalonia in Spain. If you have been to the region you no doubt have eaten it. It is similar to Crème Brulée with its caramelised sugar topping.

SERVES 6

1 litre (1¾ pints) full cream milk	8 egg yolks
1 vanilla pod and/or 1 cinnamon	200g (7oz) caster sugar
stick	3 tablespoons cornflour
zest of 1 unwaxed lemon	

- Pour the milk into a saucepan. Add the vanilla and/or cinnamon stick and the lemon zest and simmer, uncovered, for 5-10 minutes. Set aside to allow the flavours to develop.

- Meanwhile, beat the egg yolks with 125g (4oz) of the sugar and the cornflour until pale and creamy.

- Remove the vanilla pod and/or cinnamon and lemon zest from the milk and beat a ladleful into the egg mixture. Pour the egg mixture into the milk, beating well.

- Cook slowly over a low heat for 10 minutes, stirring continuously, until the mixture thickens.

- Pour into a shallow, flameproof dish and chill in the fridge for 20 minutes.

- Before serving, sprinkle the remaining sugar evenly over the top of the cream and put under a hot grill for 1 minute to caramelise.

PANNA COTTA

I adore this classical Italian dish served with apricots soaked in lemon and brandy and then puréed. Alternatively, it's good served with seasonal fruits. It's very straightforward to make and can be prepared in advance. Servings are small as it is very rich.

SERVES 4

300ml (10fl oz) double cream
2 tablespoons caster sugar or more, to taste

8 drops of vanilla essence
2 teaspoons agar agar (available from health food shops)

- Put the cream, sugar and vanilla essence in a saucepan and simmer for 2-3 minutes.

- Dissolve the agar agar in about 2 tablespoons warm water then beat well into the cream.

- Pour into 4 small bowls or dishes. Chill in the fridge for 2-3 hours, before serving.

RASPBERRY FOOL

I just had to include this recipe as it is such a favourite when raspberries are in season. I think having whole raspberries in the fool improves the taste but, if you prefer, the raspberries can be puréed before mixing with the custard to give a smooth, even-coloured fool.

SERVES 4 GENEROUSLY

450ml (¾ pint) Crème Anglaise (see page 211)	1kg (2lb) fresh raspberries
	½ teaspoon vanilla essence
150ml (¼ pint) whipping cream	mint sprigs, to decorate

- Prepare the crème anglaise as described in the recipe but cook until the custard thickens more than usual. Pour in a bowl, cover with a piece of dampened greaseproof paper and chill in the fridge for 20 minutes.

- Meanwhile, whisk the cream until it holds its shape.

- Add the raspberries, reserving a few for decoration, the cream and vanilla essence to the crème anglaise and stir together until the custard is speckled throughout with raspberries.

- Spoon the mixture into chilled serving dishes and serve decorated with the reserved raspberries and mint sprigs.

CHOCOLATE ICE CREAM

This is for chocolate lovers everywhere, particularly children. As a variation you can add 50g (2oz) chopped toasted hazelnuts and if you can't wait for it to freeze, it makes a delicious sauce.

SERVES 4

250g (8oz) plain chocolate
3 tablespoons milk
6 free range eggs, separated

4 tablespoons brandy
300ml (10fl oz) whipping cream

- Break the chocolate into a bowl and add the milk. Stand the bowl over a saucepan of simmering water and heat until melted. Remove from the heat.

- Vigorously beat in the egg yolks, one at a time then add the brandy. Leave to cool.

- Whip the cream then fold it into the mixture. Whisk the egg whites until stiff then fold them in gently.

- Pour into a freezer container and freeze for 2-3 hours until the mixture is firm.

- Remove from the freezer to soften, 1 hour before serving.

ZABAGLIONE ICE CREAM

Surprisingly, this spectacular pudding is one of the simplest to make.

SERVES 4-6

4 egg yolks	150ml (5fl oz) dry Marsala
125g (4oz) caster sugar	150ml (5fl oz) whipping cream

- Put the egg yolks into a large bowl which will fit over a saucepan. Add the sugar and whisk until the mixture is very pale and thick and leaves a trail when the beaters are lifted.

- Whisk in the Marsala, then set the bowl over a pan of simmering water and continue whisking until the mixture has at least doubled in volume.

- Remove from the heat, stand the bowl in cold water and whisk until the mixture is cool.

- Whip the cream until it just holds its shape. Add to the cold zabaglione and whisk together.

- Pour into a freezer container and freeze for about 1½ hours until firm.

- Serve in small stemmed glasses.

ESPRESSO GRANITA

I always make this coffee ice with my leftover espresso coffee. It is particularly good at 4.00pm after you have had a long, lazy lunch on a hot summer's day.

SERVES 4

75g (3oz) sugar plus 2 teaspoons coffee
450ml (¾ pint) strong expresso   225ml (8fl oz) double cream

- Add the 75g (3oz) of the sugar to the coffee and stir until dissolved. Leave to cool.

- Pour into a shallow freezer container and freeze for about 30 minutes until just beginning to set.

- Stir with a fork, stirring in the edges. Transfer to a food processor and blend quickly to break up the coffee ice.

- Return the mixture to the container and freeze for 30 minutes until firm.

- Whip the cream with the 2 teaspoons sugar until stiff.

- To serve, spoon the coffee ice into individual glasses and top with the cream.

DAMSON ICE CREAM

For flavour, damsons are the aristocrats of the plum family and make excellent ice cream. This ice cream is smooth, rich and full of flavour.

SERVES 6

450g (1lb) damsons	125g (4oz) icing sugar
125g (4oz) soft brown sugar	300ml (½ pint) double cream
4 egg yolks	2 tablespoons iced water

- Put the damsons in a saucepan with the sugar and 300ml (½ pint) of water. Bring to the boil, cover and simmer for about 10 minutes until the damsons are tender.

- Press the stewed fruit through a sieve. Chill the purée in the fridge for 20 minutes.

- Put the egg yolks and icing sugar in a bowl and stand the bowl over a saucepan of simmering water. Whisk until the mixture is warm but not hot. Remove the bowl from the heat and continue whisking until the mixture has trebled its original volume. Chill in the fridge.

- Whip the cream with the iced water until it just holds its shape. Add the damson purée, egg mixture and cream and whisk lightly together.

- Pour into a freezer container and freeze for about 1 hour until mushy.

- Turn into a chilled bowl and whisk vigorously. Return to the freezer and freeze for 2-3 hours until firm.

- Serve straight from the freezer.

BRANDY SNAP BASKETS

Serve your home-made Damson Ice Cream, or any other ice cream, in these lacy Brandy Snap Baskets.

MAKES 6

50g (2oz) butter
50g (2oz) caster sugar
2 tablespoons golden syrup or
   molasses
50g (2oz) plain flour

pinch of salt
½ teaspoon ground ginger
½ teaspoon lemon juice
1 teaspoon brandy

- Pre-heat the oven to 170°C, 325°F, Gas Mark 3. Line a baking tray with baking parchment or buttered greaseproof paper. Grease 6 inverted cups with oil.

- In a small saucepan, heat the butter, sugar and syrup or molasses until the mixture has melted and is warm but not hot.

- Sift together the flour, salt and ginger and stir them into the butter mixture. Stir in the lemon juice and brandy.

- Drop blobs (2 tablespoonfuls each) of the mixture on to the prepared baking tray, spacing each brandy snap well apart, to make 6 Brandy Snaps.

- Bake in the oven for 8-10 minutes until brown and bubbling.

- Remove from the oven and allow the brandy snaps to cool on the tray for 1 minute before lifting them, one at a time, and draping them over the oiled cups.

- Leave until set then carefully remove from the cups. Serve filled with Damson Ice Cream.

RICOTTA AND ALMOND CHEESECAKE

You will find this cheesecake in the shops throughout Italy but it is obviously better if you can make it yourself. Although it takes no time to prepare, it does take a while to cook and then cool but the result is worth the wait.

SERVES 6

a little butter, for greasing
350g (12oz) ricotta
75g (3oz) ground almonds
75g (3oz) caster sugar
6 egg yolks

grated rind and juice of 1 lemon
75g (3oz) sultanas
40g (1½oz) finely cut mixed peel
icing sugar, for dusting
seasonal fruits, to serve

- Pre-heat the oven to 180°C, 350°F, Gas Mark 4. Grease and base line an 18cm (7 inch) shallow round cake tin.

- Put the ricotta, almonds, sugar and egg yolks in a food processor and blend until smooth. Add the lemon rind and juice and blend until mixed.

- Turn the mixture into a bowl and stir in the sultanas and mixed peel. Spoon into the prepared tin and level the surface.

- Bake in the oven for about 35 minutes or until firm. Leave to cool in the tin for about 30 minutes. Turn out and serve warm or chilled, dusted with sifted icing sugar and accompanied by seasonal fruits.

PEARS COOKED IN RED WINE

This recipe always reminds me of the winter. It's particularly good served with a generous helping of mascarpone cheese. To keep all the flavour of the pears intact, don't peel them.

SERVES 4-6

800g (1¾lb) firm cooking pears
450ml (15fl oz) red wine
100g (4oz) sugar

6 whole cloves
1 cinnamon stick, halved

- Pre-heat the oven to 170°C, 325°F, Gas Mark 3.

- Core the pears and stand in an ovenproof dish. Pour over the wine, sprinkle with the sugar and add the cloves and cinnamon stick.

- Bake in the oven for 40 minutes or until the pears are tender and the liquid reduced.

- If the liquid has not reduced, remove the fruit and boil until reduced. Pour the syrup over the fruit. Serve warm or cold.

VENETIAN PUMPKIN FRITTERS

I love the many uses of pumpkin in both savoury and sweet dishes. In Italy, pumpkins are preserved in oil, char-grilled and used in risotto and pasta dishes. This sweet dish is ideal to make in autumn when pumpkins are at their very best. It is traditionally eaten before Lent, during the Carnevale in Venice, with a glass of sweet white wine.

MAKES 30

75g (3oz) sultanas
500g (1lb) pumpkin flesh
4 tablespoons caster sugar
125g (4oz) self-raising flour
1 teaspoon grated orange rind

2 eggs, separated
½ teaspoon allspice
olive oil, for deep fat frying
ground cinnamon, for dusting

- Cover the sultanas with hot water and leave for 10 minutes to soak and swell.

- Meanwhile, chop the pumpkin flesh into cubes, discarding the seeds. Put the flesh in boiling water for about 8 minutes until tender. Drain and mash in a bowl.

- Drain the sultanas and pat dry. Put in a bowl with the pumpkin, 2 tablespoon of sugar, flour, orange rind, egg yolks and allspice and mix well together.

- Whisk the egg whites until stiff then fold into the pumpkin mixture.

- Heat the oil in a saucepan and cook teaspoons of the mixture for about 8 minutes until crisp and golden. Drain on kitchen paper, toss in the remaining sugar and dust with cinnamon. Serve warm.

FLAMBE BANANAS

I nearly lost my eyebrows demonstrating this dish to a group of students. We all laughed so much at my mistake but do be careful.

SERVES 4

little butter, for greasing
4 bananas
juice of 2 oranges
25g (1oz) caster sugar

2 teaspoons cinnamon
4 tablespoons rum
extra thick double cream, to serve

- Lightly butter a flameproof dish that the bananas will fit in. Peel and arrange the bananas in the dish.

- Pour over the orange juice and sprinkle over the sugar and cinnamon. Leave in the fridge for 30 minutes.

- Pour over the rum, set alight and serve immediately with cream.

APRICOT AND PEAR CRUNCH CRUMBLE

The combination of these delicately flavoured fruits works wonderfully well in this recipe and the addition of flaked almonds gives it a lovely crunchy topping.

SERVES 6

500g (1lb) apricots
250g (8oz) pears
125g (4oz) wheatmeal (brown) flour

50g (2oz) butter or margarine
50g (2oz) soft brown sugar
125g (4oz) flaked almonds
Greek yogurt, to serve

- Pre-heat the oven to 190°C, 375°F, Gas Mark 5.

- Halve the apricots, remove the stones and put in an ovenproof dish.

- Peel and roughly chop the pears, discarding the core. Add to the apricots.

- To make the crunch crumble topping, put the flour in a bowl, add the butter or margarine and rub into the flour until the mixture resembles breadcrumbs.

- Add the sugar and almonds, mix well together and spoon over the fruit.

- Bake in the oven for 20-25 minutes until golden. Serve hot, with Greek yogurt.

LEMON TART

A Sicilian treat to die for – it is wickedly rich.

SERVES 8

1 quantity of Rich Sweet Pastry (see page 214)	100g (4oz) caster sugar
5 unwaxed lemons	50g (2oz) ground almonds
3 free range eggs	150ml (5fl oz) double cream
	icing sugar, for dusting

- Pre-heat the oven to 200°C, 400°F, Gas Mark 6.

- On a lightly floured surface, roll out the pastry and use it to line a 28cm (11 inch) flan tin. Do not remove any overhang.

- Chill the tart in the freezer for 10 minutes.

- Put the tin on a baking tray, line with foil or greaseproof paper and weigh down with baking beans. Bake blind in the oven for about 15 minutes until the sides of the pastry are crisp. Remove the lining and beans and trim the edges. Return to the oven for 5 minutes to crisp the bottom.

- Meanwhile, finely grate the rind of 2 lemons and squeeze out the juice from all the lemons. In a large bowl, beat the eggs with the sugar until it is thick and pale and leaves a trail when the beaters are lifted. Stir in the lemon rind and juice together with the almonds and cream.

- Pour the filling into the baked pastry case as soon as it comes out of the oven. Return to the oven at 180°C, 350°F, Gas Mark 4 and bake for 30 minutes until softly set.

- Pre-heat the grill. When the tart comes out of the oven, dust with icing sugar and flash under the hot grill until caramelised. Serve hot or warm.

CHOCOLATE TART

This is the richest chocolate dessert in the world!

SERVES 6-8

1 quantity of Rich Sweet Pastry (see page 214)	225g (8oz) unsalted butter
	3 whole eggs and 4 egg yolks
350g (12oz) plain chocolate	75g (3oz) caster sugar

- Pre-heat the oven to 200°C, 400°F, Gas Mark 6.

- On a lightly floured surface, roll out the pastry and use to line a 25.5cm (10 inch) flan dish or tin.

- Line the pastry case with foil or greaseproof paper and weigh down with baking beans. Bake blind in the oven for about 15 minutes until the sides of the pastry are crisp. Remove the lining and beans and return to the oven for 5 minutes until the bottom is crisp.

- Break the chocolate, cut the butter into pieces and put in a bowl, standing over a saucepan of simmering water. Heat until melted then remove from the heat.

- Using an electric whisk or mixer, beat together the eggs, egg yolks and sugar until thick and pale.

- Mix together the melted chocolate and butter, pour into the egg mixture and fold in gently. Pour the mixture into the cooked pastry case.

- Bake in the oven at 170°C, 325°F, Gas Mark 3 for 10-15 minutes until set. Leave to rest for 1 hour before serving.

ORANGE TART

Oranges are synonymous with Sicily because of the plentiful supply of sunshine. It is from there that this recipe originates and is designed to use up their abundance of oranges.

SERVES 8

1 litre (1¾ pints) freshly squeezed
    orange juice
grated rind of 4 oranges
8 free range eggs
350g (12oz) caster sugar
250ml (8fl oz) double cream

crème fraîche, to serve
For the pastry
250g (8oz) plain white flour
125g (4oz) salted butter, chilled
2 tablespoons caster sugar
1 free range egg

- Pour the orange juice into a saucepan and boil gently until reduced to 250ml (8fl oz).

- Leave the juice to cool slightly whilst making the pastry.

- To make the pastry, put the flour into a food processor. Dice the butter, add to the flour and blend until the mixture resembles breadcrumbs. Add the sugar and egg and blend until the mixture forms into a ball.

- On a floured surface, roll out the pastry and use to line a 20.5cm (8 inch) deep-sided, loose-bottomed, fluted flan tin.

- Chill the tart in the freezer for 10 minutes.

- Pre-heat the oven to 200°C, 400°F, Gas Mark 6.

- Put the tart tin on a baking tray, line with greaseproof paper or foil and weigh down with baking beans. Bake blind in the oven for 15 minutes until the sides of the pastry are crisp. Take out the lining and beans and bake for a further 5 minutes to crisp the bottom.

- Whisk together the cooled orange juice, the orange rind, eggs, sugar and cream until well mixed then pour into the pre-baked pastry case.

- Bake in the oven at 180°C, 350°F, Gas Mark 4 for 35 minutes until softly set.

- Leave to cool before serving with crème fraîche.

ORCHARD LATTICE PIE

The combination of blackberries and apples is always a firm favourite as used here in this attractive lattice pie. I often make several at one time as they freeze so well. Although overall this recipe takes time, it is mainly cooking time when you do not have to stand over it.

SERVES 6

150g (5oz) butter or margarine
300g (10oz) plain wholemeal flour
100g (4oz) soft brown sugar
1 free range egg, separated
   (optional if vegan)
grated rind and juice of 1 unwaxed
   lemon

½ teaspoon ground cinnamon
1 tablespoon semolina
700g (1½lb) cooking apples
225g (8oz) blackberries
a little caster sugar, for dusting
   (optional)

- Rub the butter or margarine into the flour until the mixture resembles breadcrumbs. Stir in 50g (2oz) of the sugar then add the egg yolk and 3 tablespoons of water (4 if omitting the egg yolk) and mix to a soft dough.

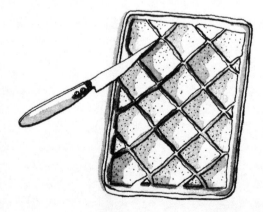

- Knead the mixture, then roll out on a floured surface to a rectangle measuring about 25 × 10cm (10 × 4 inches). Fold in three, then place the dough with the folded edges at the sides. Repeat the rolling and folding twice more. Wrap and chill in the fridge whilst preparing the filling.

- Pre-heat the oven to 200°C, 400°F, Gas Mark 6.

- To make the filling, in a bowl put the grated lemon rind, 2 tablespoons of lemon juice, the remaining 50g (2oz) of sugar, the cinnamon and semolina and stir well together.

- Peel, core and chop the apples into large pieces. Stir into the filling mixture with the blackberries.

- On a lightly floured surface, roll out two-thirds of the pastry and use to line a 19cm (7½ inch) pie plate. Pile the fruit mixture into the dish then decorate the top with a lattice made from the remaining pastry.

- Stand the dish on a baking tray and bake in the oven for about 15 minutes or until tinged with colour. If wished, remove from the oven, brush with beaten egg white and sprinkle with caster sugar. Bake for a further 25 minute, covering lightly with foil when well browned. Serve hot.

COUNTRY PEAR CAKE

Do make this cake when pears are at their best. It is simple and delicious.

SERVES 6

15g (½oz) dried breadcrumbs
11 pears
3 free range eggs
200g (7oz) caster sugar
grated rind of 1 unwaxed lemon

4 tablespoons milk
200g (oz) self raising flour
25g (1oz) butter
50g (2oz) flaked almonds

- Pre-heat the oven to 180°C, 350°F, Gas Mark 4. Grease and line a 23cm (9 inch) round cake tin and sprinkle with the breadcrumbs.

- Peel, core and slice the pears.

- In a mixing bowl, beat together the eggs, sugar and lemon rind until light and fluffy. Fold the milk and flour alternately into the mixture.

- Spoon half the mixture into the prepared tin. Arrange pear slices on top and pour over the remaining mixture. Dot with the butter and sprinkle with the almonds.

- Bake in the oven for 30-35 minutes until firm to the touch and a skewer, inserted in the centre, comes out clean. Cool on a wire rack.

ALMOND CAKE

This ancient recipe dates back to the 18th century where it was served on feast days. It is usually found in the north of Italy.

SERVES 10-12

300g (11oz) plain flour
100g (4oz) medium maize flour
250g (8oz) butter
200g (7oz) chopped blanched
   almonds

200g (7oz) caster sugar
2 free range eggs yolks
finely grated rind of 1 unwaxed
   lemon
few drops of vanilla essence

- Pre-heat the oven to 170°C, 325°F, Gas Mark 3. Grease a 23cm (9 inch) round cake tin.

- Sift the flours into a bowl. Add the butter and rub in until the mixture resembles breadcrumbs.

- Stir in the almonds, sugar, egg yolks, lemon rind and vanilla essence and mix to a smooth, stiff dough.

- Put the mixture into the prepared tin and smooth the surface.

- Bake in the oven for 45 minutes until firm to the touch. Turn out and cool on a wire rack.

APPLE CAKE

This is the best apple cake recipe I know.

SERVES 6

1-2 teaspoons vegetable oil
1-2 tablespoons dried breadcrumbs
100g (4oz) butter
700g (1½lb) Golden Delicious apples
4 free range eggs
150g (5oz) caster sugar

150g (5oz) plain flour
1 teaspoon baking powder
pinch of salt
6 tablespoons milk
finely grated rind of 1 unwaxed lemon
icing sugar, to decorate

- Pre-heat the oven to 180°C, 350°F, Gas Mark 4.

- Brush the inside of a 23cm (9 inch) round cake tin with the oil. Sprinkle with the breadcrumbs then shake off the excess.

- Melt the butter then set aside to cool.

- Core and thinly slice the apples.

- Put the eggs and sugar in a heatproof bowl, standing over a pan of gently simmering water. Whisk for 10-15 minutes until the mixture is thick and pale and leaves a trail when the beaters are lifted.

- Remove the bowl from the heat and continue whisking until the mixture is cool.

- Sift the flour with the baking powder and salt. Fold half of this mixture gently into the whisked eggs and sugar.

- Slowly trickle the melted butter around the edge of the bowl and fold it in gently. Take care not to stir too heavily or the mixture will lose its air.

- Fold in the remaining flour mixture, then the milk and lemon rind. Fold in the apples.

- Pour the cake mixture into the prepared tin. Bake in the oven for about 40 minutes until a skewer inserted into the centre comes out clean.

- Leave the cake to rest in the tin for about 5 minutes, then turn out on to a wire rack and leave to cool.

- Just before serving, sift icing sugar over the top of the cake to decorate.

SICILIAN CHOCOLATE ROLL

This recipe is rich, delicious and simple to prepare and once you have made it a few times you will like experimenting with the filling.

SERVES 8

3 free range eggs
125g (4oz) caster sugar
75g (3oz) self raising flour
2 tablespoons milk
3 tablespoons Marsala
125ml (4fl oz) double cream
50g (2oz) plain chocolate, to

decorate
For the filling
25g (1oz) dark chocolate
250g (8oz) ricotta
75g (3oz) icing sugar
½ teaspoon vanilla essence
1 tablespoon chopped glacé fruit

- Pre-heat the oven to 180°C, 350°F, Gas Mark 4. Grease and line a 25.5 × 30.5 cm (10 x 12 inch) Swiss roll tin.

- In a large mixing bowl, whisk the eggs until pale and beat until thick. Add the sugar, a little at a time, beating well after each addition, until the sugar dissolves and the mixture thickens. Fold in the flour alternatively with the milk.

- Spoon the mixture into the prepared tin. Bake in the oven for 12 minutes or until firm.

- Turn out on to a sheet of baking parchment. Remove the lining paper and trim the edges. Roll up from the narrow end, using the paper to lift and guide the roll. Leave for 5 minutes then unroll and allow to cool.

- To make the filling, grate the chocolate. Put the chocolate, ricotta, icing sugar, vanilla essence and glacé fruit in a bowl and mix together.

- Spread the filling over the cake. Re-roll and transfer to a serving plate.

- Sprinkle with the Marsala and let it soak in. Whip the cream until stiff and spread over the roll. Grate the chocolate and sprinkle over the cream to decorate.

THE RICHEST CHOCOLATE CAKE EVER

This is my best chocolate cake. Once tried it becomes everyone's favourite.

SERVES 6-8

400g (14oz) plain chocolate
100g (4oz) unsalted butter
5 free range eggs, separated
100g (4oz) caster sugar

150ml (¼ pint) double cream
icing sugar, to decorate
double cream, to serve

- Pre-heat the oven to 180°C, 350°F, Gas Mark 4. Grease and flour a 25.5cm (10 inch) round loose-bottomed cake tin.

- Break the chocolate into a bowl and add the butter. Stand the bowl over a saucepan of simmering water and heat until melted.

- Whisk together the egg yolks and sugar until thick and pale.

- Whisk the egg whites until stiff.

- Add the chocolate mixture to the egg yolks then add the cream and mix well together. Fold in the egg whites.

- Pour the mixture into the prepared tin and bake in the oven for 25 minutes. The cake will still be wobbly. Don't worry – all is fine as the cake will set as it cools.

- Serve with a dusting of icing sugar and cream.

APPLE SLICE

I ate this at Gianni Gosett's Ristorante Roma at Tolmezzo in the mountains and so enjoyed it, that I include it here.

SERVES 6-8

For the pastry
250g (8oz) white flour
50g (2oz) caster sugar
grated rind of ½ a lemon
150g (5oz) unsalted butter
1 tablespoon rum
1-2 tablespoons milk, if necessary
For the filling
750g (1½lb) sweet eating apples,
such as Cox's orange Pippins
75g (3oz) sugar
50g (2oz) raisins
4 tablespoons rum
2 teaspoons cinnamon
juice of 1 small unwaxed lemon
100g (4oz) ground walnuts,
hazelnuts or almonds
icing sugar, to decorate

- To make the pastry, in a bowl, mix together the flour, sugar and lemon rind. Cut the butter into small pieces and rub into the flour until the mixture resembles fine breadcrumbs. Add the rum and work briefly with your hands into a soft dough, adding the extra milk only if necessary. Wrap the pastry in cling film and let it rest in the fridge for 20 minutes.

- Meanwhile, peel, core and slice the apples then mix together with all the filling ingredients.

- Pre-heat the oven to 180°C, 350°F, Gas Mark 4.

- Divide the pastry into two, one of them slightly larger, and form each into a ball. On a well floured surface, roll out the larger ball and use to line a 25.5-30.5cm (10-12 inch) flan tin.

- Spread the filling on top and cover with the remaining pastry, rolled out thinly. With a fork, lightly prick the surface.

- Bake in the oven for about 35 minutes until pale golden. Serve sprinkled with icing sugar.

ALMOND MACAROONS

This is one of my most requested recipes hence my reason for including it here. Wrapped in cellophane and tied with a pretty ribbon, they make an excellent gift.

MAKES ABOUT 24

225g (8oz) ground almonds	2 egg whites
225g (8oz) unrefined caster sugar	1 teaspoon almond essence

- Pre-heat the oven to 180°C, 350°F, Gas Mark 4. Dust baking trays with flour or line with rice paper.

- Mix together the almonds and sugar.

- In a large bowl, whisk the egg whites until stiff but not dry. Gradually fold in the almond and sugar mixture then add the almond essence.

- Pipe or spoon the mixture on to the prepared baking trays.

- Bake in the oven for 15-20 minutes until golden brown. Transfer the cooked macaroons to a cooling rack. They should be crisp on the outside but with a rather chewy centre. Longer cooking will crisp them all the way through if liked. Transfer to a wire rack and leave to cool.

ORANGE ALMOND COOKIES

These are very good wrapped in cellophane. They make an excellent present.

MAKES 12

100g (4oz) ground almonds	100g (4oz) plain flour
100g (4oz) caster sugar	about 6 tablespoons milk
100g (4oz) candied orange peel	50g (2oz) plain chocolate

- Pre-heat the oven to 180°C, 350°F, Gas Mark 4. Line several baking trays with parchment paper.

- Put the almonds, sugar and orange peel in a bowl. Sift in the flour, reserving 1 tablespoon, and mix well together. Add enough milk to form a smooth, firm dough.

- Roll the mixture into 24 small balls and place well apart on the baking trays. Sprinkle with the remaining flour.

- Bake in the oven for 15 minutes until golden brown. Transfer to a wire rack and leave to cool.

- Melt the chocolate and use a little to sandwich the cookies together in pairs.

ALMOND SHORTBREAD

This recipe is from my Italian friends in Verona. It is delicious and really does melt in the mouth.

MAKES ABOUT 2.5KG (5½LB)

25g (1oz) unblanched almonds
25g (1oz) ground almonds
100g (4oz) plain wholemeal flour
100g (4oz) plain white flour

75g (3oz) caster sugar
½ teaspoon ground ginger
225g (8oz) butter
icing sugar, for sprinkling

- Pre-heat the oven to 180°C, 350°F, Gas Mark 4.

- Finely chop the unblanched almonds and put in a bowl. Add the ground almonds, wholemeal and plain flour, the caster sugar and ground ginger and mix together.

- Cut up the butter, add to the flour mixture and rub in until the mixture resembles fine breadcrumbs then draw the mixture together to form a ball.

- On a lightly floured baking tray, roll out the mixture into a round, 0.5cm (¼ inch) thick. Cut into 8 sections.

- Bake in the oven for 40 minutes until pale golden. Dust with sifted icing sugar and leave to cool on the tray. Store in an airtight container.

PEACH JAM

Succulent and flavoursome, this jam will bring back golden memories of summer.

MAKES ABOUT 2.5KG (5½LB)

1 medium cooking apple	1.5kg (3lb) peaches
pared rind of 2 lemons	1 teaspoon ground allspice
2 whole cloves	1kg (2lb) granulated sugar

- Finely chop the apple and put in a double piece of muslin with the lemon rind and cloves.

- Cut the peaches in half then slice, discarding the stones. Put the peaches, 300ml (½ pint) water and the muslin bag in a preserving pan. Bring to the boil, stirring continuously, then reduce the heat and simmer for about 30 minutes, stirring frequently, until the peaches are just soft.

- Remove the muslin bag and press it against the side of the pan with a wooden spoon to extract as much juice as possible.

- Add the allspice and sugar and stir until the sugar has dissolved. Bring the mixture to the boil and boil rapidly for 15-20 minutes, stirring frequently, until setting point is reached. (To tell when setting point has been reached, place a teaspoonful of the hot jam on to a saucer and place in the fridge for 3 minutes. Take it out and using your finger push the surface of the jam. If it wrinkles the mixture has reached setting point.) Set aside for 10 minutes.

- Pour into clean, hot, sterilised jars and cover.

BANANA CURD

This recipe is taken from The 90's Vegetarian. *It really is a sweet treat! It is quick to make and excellent on toast, bagels, scones and pancakes. It also makes use of ripe bananas.*

MAKES ABOUT TWO 450G (1LB) JARS

4 large bananas
125g (4oz) unsalted butter
250g (8oz) caster sugar
grated rind and juice of 1 unwaxed

lemon
generous pinch of ground ginger or
1 teaspoon chopped fresh ginger
4 large free range eggs

- Put the bananas in a bowl and mash.

- Melt the butter in a saucepan then add the sugar, bananas, lemon rind and juice and ginger. Cook gently for 10 minutes.

- Beat the eggs in a bowl then gradually beat in 3 tablespoons of the banana mixture. Pour into the banana mixture and stir well. Cook gently, stirring constantly, for 10 minutes or until the mixture coats the back of a wooden spoon. Do not boil.

- Pour into hot, sterilised jars and cover. Store in the fridge and eat within 10 days.

Glossary of Essential Recipes

These are the recipes that you will turn to again and again. I have collected them together in this chapter to avoid repetition and for easy reference. Here you will find sauces, stock, pastries and instructions for cooking pasta. All can be prepared in advance, saving you valuable cooking time.

BECHAMEL SAUCE

MAKES ABOUT 750ML (1¼ PINTS)

50g (2oz) butter
100g (4oz) plain flour
750ml (1¼ pints) milk

freshly grated nutmeg
salt and pepper

- Melt the butter in a medium saucepan. Remove from the heat and add the flour, stirring continuously with a wooden spoon to form a smooth paste.

- Add 4 tablespoons of milk and stir well together. Add another 4 tablespoons of milk and stir until completely smooth.

- Return to the heat and gradually stir in the remaining milk. Season with nutmeg, salt and pepper.

- Bring to the boil and continue cooking, stirring, until the sauce thickens and coats the back of the wooden spoon.

CHEESE SAUCE

MAKES ABOUT 750ML (1¼ PINTS)

50g (2oz) hard cheese, of your choice
50g (2oz) butter
100g (4oz) plain flour
750ml (1¼ pints) milk

salt and pepper
handful of chopped fresh herbs, such as parsley, thyme, marjoram (optional)

- Grate the cheese.

- Melt the butter in a saucepan. Stir in the flour to form a smooth paste. Remove from the heat.

- Gradually stir in the milk until smooth. Return to the heat and slowly bring to the boil, stirring constantly, until the sauce boils and thickens. Season with salt and pepper to taste.

- Stir the cheese and herbs, if using, into the cooked sauce until the cheese has melted.

TOMATO SAUCE

MAKES ABOUT 300ML (½ PINT)

450g (1lb) ripe fresh tomatoes or a 400g can tomatoes
1 small onion
1 garlic clove
1 tablespoon olive oil
150ml (¼ pint) Vegetable Stock or water (see page 209)

1 tablespoon tomato purée
pinch of sugar
handful of torn fresh basil leaves (optional)
salt and pepper
1 tablespoon dry white wine

- If using fresh tomatoes, put in a bowl, cover with boiling water for about 30 seconds then plunge into cold water. Using a sharp knife, peel off the skins then roughly chop the flesh, discarding the seeds.

- Finely chop the onion and crush the garlic. Heat the oil in a saucepan, add the onion and cook gently for 5 minutes until softened.

- Add the tomatoes and garlic, cover and cook over a gentle heat for 10 minutes, stirring occasionally.

- Add the stock or water, tomato purée, sugar, basil if using, and salt and pepper to taste. Half cover the pan and simmer for 20 minutes, stirring occasionally.

- Sieve the tomato mixture into a clean pan. Bring to the boil, add the wine then use as required.

MINTED YOGURT SAUCE

MAKES 300ML (½ PINT)

300ml (½ pint) natural yogurt	2 teaspoons fresh lemon juice
handful of chopped fresh mint	salt and pepper

- Put all the ingredients in a bowl and whisk together until well blended.
- Chill before serving.

ITALIAN DRESSING

SERVES 4

4 tablespoons extra virgin olive oil	lemon juice
2 tablespoons freshly squeezed	salt and pepper

- Put all the ingredients in a bowl and whisk together until well blended.

- Use as required.

LEMON AND PARMESAN CHEESE DRESSING

SERVES 4-6

juice of 1 unwaxed lemon
4 tablespoons fruity extra virgin
   olive oil

2 tablespoons freshly grated
   Parmesan cheese
salt and pepper

- Put all the ingredients in a bowl and whisk together until well blended and thick.

- Use as required.

VEGETABLE STOCK

MAKES 1 LITRE (2 PINTS)

1 garlic clove	40g (1½oz) unsalted butter
2 onions	1 tablespoon olive oil
6 carrots	4 bay leaves
4 leeks	2 sprigs of fresh thyme
2 celery sticks	handful of flat-leaved fresh parsley
12 whole cloves	salt and pepper

- Chop the garlic, 1 onion, the carrots, leeks and celery. Skin the remaining onion and stud with the cloves.

- In a large, heavy based saucepan, melt the butter with the oil. Add the garlic and fry for 2 minutes. Add the chopped onion, carrots, leeks, celery and whole onion and cook for 5-7 minutes until softened, stirring continuously.

- Add 3 litres (5¼ pints) of water, the bay leaves, thyme, parsley, salt and pepper. Bring to the boil, cover and simmer for 1½ hours.

- Remove from the heat and leave to cool for 1½ hours.

- Return the pan to the heat and simmer for 15 minutes.

- Strain the stock through a sieve and return to the pan. Boil rapidly until reduced by half.

- Allow to cool completely then store in the fridge for up to 3 days.

COOKING PASTA

SERVES 4

400g (14oz) fresh or dried pasta   salt (optional)

- Bring a large, deep saucepan of water to the boil (allow 1 litre/1¾ pints to 100g/4oz pasta), adding salt if wished.

- Add the pasta, return to the boil then cook fresh pasta for 4 minutes, dried pasta according to the instructions on the packet or until just tender.

- Turn the pasta into a colander and drain well.

- Serve immediately, tossed in a knob of butter, 1 tablespoon olive oil, with a sauce or according to individual recipes.

CREME ANGLAISE

MAKES 450ML (¾ PINT)

450ml (¾ pint) milk	½ teaspoon salt
4 large egg yolks	1 teaspoon vanilla essence
6 tablespoons caster sugar	little grated lemon rind (optional)

- In a saucepan, bring the milk to just below boiling point and keep it hot.

- In a bowl, whisk together the egg yolks, sugar and salt until pale and fluffy.

- Stirring, with a wooden spoon, pour in the hot milk. Return the mixture to the pan and heat gently, stirring frequently, until it thickens and coats the back of a wooden spoon.

- Stir in the vanilla essence and lemon rind, if using. Serve as a hot sauce or use as part of a recipe.

SHORTCRUST PASTRY

MAKES 375G (12OZ)

250g (8oz) plain white flour   125g (4oz) cold butter
pinch of salt

- Put the flour and salt in a food processor. Cut up the butter, add to the flour and blend for 1 minute. Alternatively, put the flour and salt in a large bowl. Cut up the butter and rub in with your fingertips until the mixture resembles fine breadcrumbs.

- Add 2-3 tablespoons cold water to bind the mixture together.

- Wrap and chill in the fridge for 15 minutes before use.

ROUGH PUFF PASTRY

MAKES 400G (1LB)

250g (8oz) plain flour	75g (3oz) butter or margarine
pinch of salt	75g (3oz) hard white vegetable fat

- Sift the flour and salt into a bowl. Add the butter or margarine and vegetable fat and cut into 1cm (½ inch) pieces using 2 round bladed knives in a scissor action.

- Gradually stir in 150ml (¼ pint) cold water to make a soft dough.

- Turn the dough on to a lightly floured surface and knead until smooth then roll out to a rectangle measuring 30.5 × 12.5 cm (12 × 5 inches).

- Fold the top third down and the bottom third up then turn so that the folded edges are at the sides. Repeat the rolling and folding 3 more times.

- Wrap in greaseproof paper and chill in the fridge for at least 20 minutes before using.

RICH SWEET PASTRY

MAKES 475G (1LB)

250g (8oz) plain white flour
75g (3oz) icing sugar
125g (4oz) butter
1 large free range egg

pinch of salt
few drops of vanilla essence
grated rind of 1 unwaxed lemon

- Sift the flour and icing sugar into a bowl and rub in the butter until the mixture resembles breadcrumbs.

- Make a well in the centre and add the egg, salt, vanilla essence and lemon rind.

- Gradually work the flour in from the edges and mix to a smooth dough.

- Wrap in greaseproof paper and leave to rest in the fridge for about 30 minutes before using.

The Cook's Own Pages

Use these pages to note your favourite recipes, adaptions you've made to them and to keep a record of the recipes you have served when entertaining.

Index